"Dads, do you ever struggle to find creaf time with your daughter? If so, *88 Gr* offers some great ideas. This book will the most of the time you have with her."

—**Kirk Cameron**, actor

"From the second I learned about Rob Teigen's newest book, *88 Great Daddy-Daughter Dates*, I knew I would be purchasing copies for my sons-in-law. Rob makes it easy for dads and daughters to spend time together. He provides the ideas, the encouragement, and the reasons that will reap blessings in every dad/daughter relationship."

—**Elizabeth George**, author of *A Woman After God's Own Heart* and *Raising a Daughter After God's Own Heart*

"*88 Great Daddy-Daughter Dates* is a fantastic way to affirm your daughter and to invest in her as she prepares for womanhood. A wise father will take advantage of these ideas to nurture her and to capture her heart. This book is brilliant!"

—**Alex Kendrick**, writer/director of *Fireproof* and *Courageous*

"What a wonderful, needed book. If fathers lived out the ideas in this book, their daughters would feel loved and secure, and would make better choices in their teen years.

—**Rebecca St. James**, singer, author, actress

"Wow! This book hits it out of the park, in my opinion. For any dad who wants to raise a daughter who knows she is loved and treasured, *88 Great Daddy-Daughter Dates* is the book for you! Finally, a straightforward tool that will equip dads to invest spiritually, love intentionally, and connect emotionally with their daughters. One of my favorite books this year!"

—**Lysa TerKeurst**, *New York Times* bestselling author of *Made to Crave*

"I love my girls and have grabbed every opportunity to connect with them in meaningful ways. Having fun and spending one-on-one time together creates memories and makes an impact that lasts a lifetime. If you want to capture the heart of your daughter, this book is a great place to start!"

—**Dr. Kevin Leman**, *New York Times* bestselling author of *What a Difference a Daddy Makes* and *Have a New Kid by Friday*

"Some of my most treasured moments and memories of my life have been special dates with my daughters. Rob and Joanna mix fun, bonding, and incredible spiritual connection with every date. Your daughter will thank you over and over again and treasure every moment, as you will too."

—**Jim Burns**, PhD, president of HomeWord and author of *Teen-ology*, *The Art of Raising Great Teens* and *The Purity Code*

"When my daughter was growing up, we loved spending time together (now that she's 23, we still do, but things have changed!). Sometimes the simplest things were the best: hitting the swings at school, walking along a creek, or our favorite, eating yogurt! How I would have cherished a book like this back then, not only to aid my creativity, but also to remind me to use these moments as a time we shared with Jesus. What a great idea; what a great book."

—**Chap Clark**, PhD, Vice Provost of Regional Campuses, Fuller Theological Seminary, and author of *Hurt 2.0: Inside the World of Today's Teenagers*

"In today's increasingly complicated and busy world, dads are looking for ways to connect with their daughters. In this wonderful resource, Rob and Joanna provide practical and fun ways dads can stay involved in their daughters' lives. Dads will use this book to create memories and build bridges of communication that will last a lifetime. Dads are the most influential men in their girls' lives and will shape how their daughters view themselves, other men, and even God. If you're the father of a daughter, get this book!"

—**Carey Casey**, CEO, National Center for Fathering; fathers.com

"Wow—what a great book! Rob and Joanna Teigen flat-out nailed it in describing the path to a girl's heart. Guys, are you stumped about how to connect with your daughter? If you do even a tenth of the ideas in this book, you'll have a little girl who adores her daddy—guaranteed! I wish Rob Teigen was my dad—and I'm not even a girl."

—**Rick Johnson**, bestselling author of *That's My Son*; *Better Dads, Stronger Sons*; and *That's My Girl*

"As a self-professed 'daddy's girl' I can relate to Rob Teigen's wonderful, fun-filled book of ideas for dates with fathers and their girls. The father/daughter bond is an important one, and there's no one who can provide a better example of how a girl should be treated on a date than her own daddy—the first man in her life. Dads, *88 Great Daddy-Daughter Dates* will help you create memories to last a lifetime!"

—**Carol M. Mackey**, author of the bestselling *Sistergirl Devotions: Keeping Jesus in the Mix on the Job*

"I'm excited for dads to have this 'by the numbers' guide for spending time with their daughters. Keep up the good work!"

—**Jim George**, author of *Man After God's Own Heart*

88 GREAT DADDY-DAUGHTER DATES

Fun, Easy & Creative Ways
to Build Memories Together

Rob and Joanna Teigen

Revell
a division of Baker Publishing Group
Grand Rapids, Michigan

© 2012 by Rob and Joanna Teigen

Published by Revell
a division of Baker Publishing Group
P.O. Box 6287, Grand Rapids, MI 49516-6287
www.revellbooks.com

Printed in the United States of America

Library of Congress Cataloging-in-Publication Data
Teigen, Rob.
    88 great daddy-daughter dates : fun, easy & creative ways to build memories together / Rob and Joanna Teigen.
        p.   cm.
    ISBN 978-0-8007-2033-9 (pbk.)
    1. Fathers and daughters—Religious aspects—Christianity. I. Teigen, Joanna. II. Title.
    BV4529.17.T45 2011
    248.8′421—dc23   2011041153

14   15   16   17   18   7   6   5

To Josh, Emma, Leah, and Anna

It is a privilege to be your mom and dad.
You are our greatest blessings and we're crazy about you!

Contents

Introduction

Why a daddy-daughter date book? It all started when I met my wife, Joanna. I remember the restaurants, the flowers, the love notes, and the talking (*all* the talking). She loved it and fell for me since I was such a romantic guy. This was perfect—she married me and I was set!

Well, I believe we men often relax from all that relationship stuff after the "I do" and go back to life as usual. No more flowers, love notes, dinners out—and definitely less talking. I've spent my share of nights in bed looking at my wife's back as she radiated silent misery over being shut out and ignored. Note to self: date my wife!

You may be saying, "Well, duh, Einstein." But cut me a break. The whole "girl" thing was new to me. I was raised in a home with four boys. We collectively crushed my mom's attempts to preserve a feminine touch in the house (I remember her weeping as her last collectible plate was smashed by one of us boys during an indoor water fight).

Joanna and I were married for almost two years when we were blessed with our first child, Josh. It was a good thing we had a boy first; God knew I still had a lot to learn about girls before he could trust me with a daughter. After a few years, he tried a new strategy to teach me about females: full immersion! He has blessed me with three daughters, and now I'm learning more about girls each day than I ever imagined.

Emma, Leah, and Anna have won my heart. They make me want to be the best husband and father I can be. I've spent hours on my knees praying and many more hours scratching my head, thinking, *I don't know if I understand these creatures, but the joy they bring makes it worth the effort to try!*

I found the passion to connect with my daughters, but not the tools. I also discovered that dads I knew felt just like me: they loved their little girls but felt ill-equipped to connect with them on a deeper level, especially in this fast-paced world where girls grow up way too fast.

The pressure is on—I read over and over how significant a dad's relationship with his daughter is to her emotional and spiritual well-being. You're going to be the first important and influential man in your daughter's life. Kevin Leman says in his book *What a Difference a Daddy Makes*:

> A woman's relationship with her father, more than any other relationship, is going to affect her relationship with all other males in her life—her bosses, coworkers, subordinates, sons, husbands, brothers, pastors, college professors, and even Hollywood movie stars. (You tell me if a woman chooses Dennis Rodman over Michael Jordan, and I'll give you an accurate picture of her father!) There's not a single relationship that isn't indelibly stamped—for good or for ill—by the man known as Daddy.[1]

So many voices in our culture are calling out for girls' affections. A strong relationship with your daughter can direct her heart and mind toward the right influences, and ultimately toward a relationship with God. Chap and Dee Clark, in their book *Daughters and Dads*, say:

1. Kevin Leman, *What a Difference a Daddy Makes* (Nashville: Thomas Nelson, 2000), 5.

Daughters in today's world need mothers and fathers who are willing to trust God's creative handiwork when it comes to their identity. Society cannot dictate who your daughter is to be, nor is the church called to handle the task. Instead, a daughter needs a few select people in her life who have the conviction and ability to help her become the person God created her to be.[2]

My hope is this date book will help you do that in some small way.

So many voices surrounding our daughters tell them what they're not: not thin enough, not stylish enough, not smart enough, not athletic enough, not, not, not. A dad can communicate to his daughter who she truly is: a beautiful child of a God who created her intentionally, has plans for her, and loves her with all his heart. This message is conveyed through time spent together, where affirmation, fun experiences, meaningful conversations, and prayers happen.

I don't know about you, but no guy is good enough for any of my daughters. The boy that comes along who is interested in my little girl had better be a respectful, trustworthy, kind, and godly man if he even thinks he's going to have a shot at dating her. That's how I feel, but I had better parent my daughters in a way that models how they deserve to be loved. Then they won't want to settle for less—they'll wait for the young man who is worthy of holding their hearts. By developing a pattern of loving, intentional fathering, you will shape her standard for relationships for a lifetime.

There are two primary challenges when it comes to spending time with our daughters: first, making it happen. Second, making the time meaningful.

We all struggle with making it happen as we fall victim to the "I'll do it next week" syndrome. Be intentional with your plans. Choose specific times to spend with your daughter, write them on your calendar, and stick to the plan as best you can. If you need to reschedule due to an unexpected conflict, put a new date on the

2. Chap Clark and Dee Clark, *Daughters and Dads* (Colorado Springs: Nav Press, 1998), 88.

calendar right away. This will assure your daughter of your commitment to spend time with her.

Dates with your daughter need to be not just entertaining but significant as well. You want to create an environment where you can hear how she's doing and listen to her as she opens up.

This book is designed to help you with both of those elements. The "Grab" and "Go" sections listed for each date will help you plan your time and make it happen. You'll get lists of supplies, find out if spending money is needed, and see if it's an at-home activity or an outing. The "Grow" section of each date helps you connect on a deeper level with each other and with God. You'll find questions to talk about, thoughts to share, Scriptures to read, and prayers to wrap up your time together. The last eight date ideas are "extreme dates," which are special activities that require more planning or expense than a typical date. They also allow for a more significant amount of time together.

Another important element to your daddy-daughter dates actually involves your marriage: make sure you commit to dating your wife first. Not only does this keep your marriage relationship in first place, it sets an example for your daughter of what a loving, committed relationship looks like. Her trust in you will grow as she sees you love her mom. As she sees you treat your wife like a queen, she'll thrive in her role of "princess" even more!

My wife is a key element in the success of my relationships with my girls. That's one of the reasons I asked if she would write this book with me. (Aside from the fact that she's a better writer than me too!) She has been supportive as I block out time in our busy schedules to spend with our girls. She has expressed that my relationship with both her and our children are entwined. She feels loved when I invest in our family, and our daughters feel valued as girls when I honor their mom. Include your wife in setting up a date schedule and planning your outings. She will have creative input and suggestions that can make your time with your daughter even more wonderful.

The dates in this book include a variety of indoor and outdoor, quiet and active, and seasonal and holiday-oriented activities. Some of the suggestions might not be your "thing," but be brave and try a few anyway. If a date is just not flowing well or you run into obstacles like thunderstorms or car trouble, just drop everything and get some ice cream. (Ice cream is an integral part of both the Teigen family and this book. If you're lactose intolerant, this may not be the book for you!) Stay flexible and remember that the dates are just tools, not rules. Your daughter won't care if you are following the date to the letter—she just wants time with you.

I pray for God's blessing on each dad who uses this book to connect with his daughter. May you find joy in winning her heart!

Rob

Like Rob mentioned in his introduction, I do find that his dates with our girls benefit our whole family. When Rob dates me or any of our kids, he is saying, "You are important. You deserve my time and attention. I'm crazy about you!" We come home from time with him feeling valued and heard as he gives us his undivided attention. My girls carry those feelings into the rest of their lives, where I see them growing in confidence and self-respect.

Rob has made a deep impact on our daughters' relationships with God as well. They assume their heavenly Father is as gentle and attentive as their earthly father. They expect to be heard when they pray. They believe God is on their side and loves them as daughters. Rob's love for them is their first taste of the love of God himself, and of course they want to know him more!

It does take some juggling to fit in frequent one-on-one time with each child. I see my role as "date facilitator," making sure our schedules are in sync and the girls are ready to head out the door. Sometimes I'll help out with the prep for the dates—getting cash, tickets, or snacks prepared in advance. I'm happy to help out when I can, since the payoff is worth it!

I'm a wife who is loved very well. It is a thrill for me to see my daughters being cared for so deeply by my husband. When I look to the future, I know my girls will understand what real love looks like and not want to settle for less.

Have an amazing time dating your daughter. I praise God for all he has planned for each of you!

Joanna

10 Tips for a Successful Daddy-Daughter Date

1. Have fun—leave your cares behind and just focus on your daughter.

2. As much as possible keep that Smartphone put away. Don't try to talk to your daughter and text, answer email, or surf the Web at the same time.

3. Really listen to your daughter. Don't be too quick to give your opinion or "fix" her issues. Seek to understand her more than to be understood.

4. Don't be afraid to redo or scrap a date that isn't working. As you know, with kids there are moods involved and different personalities. If you've had an awesome time, though, try that date again and again!

5. BE YOU! You don't have to pretend to *love* shopping at the mall. And she doesn't have to be thrilled about a football game. If the focus is on your time with each other rather than the "entertainment," it's all good.

6. Don't be overly task-oriented. The goal is to connect with your daughter, not get through every detail in the book.

7. You'll get more comfortable with all the material and dates the more you do them.

8. Set a goal to learn something new about your daughter every time you go out together.

9. Before you go out on your dates, pray that God will prepare both your hearts for the conversations you'll have and the memories you'll create.

10. Build anticipation. Let your daughter know ahead of time that you're excited about spending time with her. Let her know it's a big deal to you.

1
Flip a Coin

☞ Grab

» Coin
» Your daughter's favorite "road music"

» Digital timer or egg timer
» Car keys
» Money

Go

Buckle up in the car with your daughter and give her the coin. Pop in a CD or set your MP3 player to some favorite music. If she asks where you're going, well, you have no idea! Begin driving down your street and ask your daughter to flip the coin. If the coin lands on heads, take the next right turn. If the coin lands on tails, take the next left turn. Set your timer for three minutes. When the timer goes off, have your daughter flip the coin again. If it lands on heads, take another right turn; tails mean another left. Repeat this every three minutes for about half an hour.

During your drive time, don't worry if you find yourselves driving in circles—that's part of the fun. Use this time to talk about her week at school, plans for your next family vacation, or any funny stories you have to share about school or work.

At the end of your half hour of driving, see where you have arrived! Find the nearest place around you to stop for a soda or ice cream.

🌱 Grow

Life is full of surprises! Sometimes we can't make heads or tails out of what is going on. The Lord is the only one who knows the future, and he usually only shows us a little bit of his plan at a time. Ask your daughter these questions:

> » Did it make you feel stressed out when you didn't know where you were going?
> » Did you feel relaxed because you knew your dad was in the driver's seat?
> » Was it hard to sit back and enjoy the ride instead of just focusing on the destination?
> » Have you ever felt worried because you didn't know how a situation would turn out?
> » Was it ever hard to make a decision because you didn't know what the outcome would be?

> The father of a daughter is nothing but a high-class hostage. A father turns a stony face to his sons, berates them, shakes his antlers, paws the ground, snorts, runs them off into the underbrush, but when his daughter puts her arm over his shoulder and says, "Daddy, I need to ask you something," he is a pat of butter in a hot frying pan.
>
> Garrison Keillor

Share with your daughter about a time when you were worried about the future or had a tough choice to make. Describe how God took care of you in that situation or helped you with that decision. It can be a challenge to trust our heavenly Father with the future. Read and talk about these verses together:

> Trust in the LORD with all your heart,
> and do not lean on your own understanding.
> In all your ways acknowledge him,
> and he will make straight your paths. (Prov. 3:5–6 ESV)

> Make me to know your ways, O LORD;
> teach me your paths.
> Lead me in your truth and teach me,
> for you are the God of my salvation;
> for you I wait all the day long. (Ps. 25:4–5 ESV)

Dear Father,

We thank you for being in the driver's seat of our lives. You are all-knowing and all-powerful, so we know you can handle anything that comes our way. Please teach us to trust you when hard things happen or we don't know what to do. Help us to be patient when we're anxious to know the future. Show us how to follow you every day. Amen!

2

There's No One Like You

☞ Grab

» Old magazines
» Computer and printer
» Scissors and glue sticks

» Poster board
» Markers

Go

Your daughter is a unique masterpiece, created by God. Today you will create your own work of art to celebrate your one-of-a-kind girl!

Use your computer's word processing software to spell out "All About (your daughter's name)." Have your daughter choose her favorite font and color for the lettering. Print and cut out the title you've made and glue it across the top of the poster board. Page through old magazines or search the internet together to find pictures of your daughter's interests and favorite things: sports, colors, foods, stores, movies, animals, fashions, etc. Cut out or print the pictures and glue them onto the poster board.

When you're finished cutting and pasting, use markers to embellish the poster. Write down words that describe the qualities of your daughter's heart and personality (funny, helpful, generous, friendly, confident, honest, etc.).

Find a place on your daughter's bedroom door or wall to display the poster, to celebrate what a unique and special girl she is.

〽️ Grow

Take some time to study the finished poster together. Ask specific questions about the pictures she chose, such as, "What do you like best about that animal?" or "What was your favorite part of that movie?" This is a great opportunity to get to know her better.

Your daughter was created by God and he knows her through and through. The pictures she chose to place on the poster show how she already has talents and interests that make her unique, despite her young age. The qualities of her heart and personality, however, are where the fingerprint of God is especially evident. Read the following verses together:

> O Lord, you have searched me and known me!
> You know when I sit down and when I rise up;
> you discern my thoughts from afar.
> You search out my path and my lying down
> and are acquainted with all my ways. (Ps. 139:1–3 ESV)
>
> For you formed my inward parts;
> you knitted me together in my mother's womb.
> I praise you, for I am fearfully and wonderfully made.
> Wonderful are your works;
> my soul knows it very well. (vv. 13–14 ESV)

Dear Lord,

No other girl is quite like my daughter. Thank you for creating her and knowing her through and through. I am so grateful that you made her just the way she is. Thank you for what a gift she is to me and our family. Please help her to trust in your amazing love for her, and help me to love her the way you do. Amen!

3

Putt-Putt and Pictures

☞ Grab

- » Camera
- » Your daughter's favorite candies
- » Car keys
- » Money

Go

I love putt-putt with my daughter—it's the one time when I feel like I'm golfing with someone at my level! Travel to a mini-golf course. Let your daughter choose the ball colors for each of you. Have fun taking pictures of each other as you make your way through each hole. Reward yourselves with a piece of candy for each successful putt into the hole. Choose a special prize for a hole-in-one!

> **Dad to Dad**
> *If the competition of the game is creating stress for your daughter, consider throwing out the scorecard altogether. Or make it a team effort by taking turns with the same putter and working on each hole together.*

⚜ Grow

Did you make a hole-in-one every time? Of course not! We don't make a "hole-in-one" for every situation in life either. It can be hard when we don't get an A on the test, win the game, or get invited to someone's party. Sometimes we let our friends down, disobey our parents, and have a crummy attitude. What do we do? Give up and quit playing the game of life? Or go to God for forgiveness and strength and try the "putt" again?

Dad, share with your daughter about a time you failed or let someone down. Explain how God used it to teach you something and what steps you took to make it right.

God is a God of second (and third and fourth and fifth!) chances. Read these verses together:

> The steadfast love of the LORD never ceases;
> his mercies never come to an end;
> They are new every morning;
> great is your faithfulness. (Lam. 3:22–23 ESV)

> For you, O Lord, are good and forgiving,
> abounding in steadfast love to all who call upon you.
>   (Ps. 86:5 ESV)

There is therefore now no condemnation for those who are in Christ Jesus. For the law of the Spirit of life has set you free in Christ Jesus from the law of sin and death. (Rom. 8:1–2 ESV)

Dear God,

Thank you for forgiving us for all our sins. Thank you that there's nothing we could ever do that would keep you from loving us. Thank you for never giving up on us even when we sin over and over again. Help us to learn from our mistakes. Give us the courage to admit when we're wrong. And help us to come to you for forgiveness and a fresh start every time. We love you! Amen.

4

Puppy Love

☞ Grab

» Money
» Car keys
» Camera

Go

Travel to your local pet store. Have a great time exploring the different departments. Check out the dogs and cats, the turtles and lizards, the hamsters and parakeets, and the tanks of fish. Allow your daughter to take pictures of the animals she thinks are cute or funny. Observe the animals together and ask your daughter if any of them seem nervous. Do some of them seem sad or bored? Cute and friendly? Aggressive? Shy? Talk with the staff, if possible, about where the various animals come from and which are their favorites to care for.

When you're done with your visit for the day, make your way to a toy store so your daughter can "adopt" a new stuffed animal as a keepsake of your time together.

> **Dad to Dad**
> *This date is not for the faint of heart! For some little girls, visiting a pet store will pull too hard on the heartstrings, resulting in tears and begging for a new pet. Tread carefully, my fellow dads!*

🌱 Grow

It is hard to imagine the feeling of being all alone in the world. Your daughter has a place where she belongs—in your heart and home. Ask her how she thinks it would feel to be an animal in a pet store, in an unfamiliar place with loud noises, odd smells, and strangers all around her.

The Bible says that before we know Christ we are lost too. We don't have hope or any certainty about the future. But out of God's amazing love he adopts us and calls us his children. We have a wonderful Father who never lets us go and promises a forever home for us. Doesn't it feel good to know that we belong to a Father like that, and have an amazing home in heaven to look forward to?

Read these verses together:

See what kind of love the Father has given to us, that we should be called children of God; and so we are. (1 John 3:1 ESV)

My sheep hear my voice, and I know them, and they follow me. I give them eternal life, and they will never perish, and no one will snatch them out of my hand. My Father, who has given them to me, is greater than all, and no one is able to snatch them out of the Father's hand. (John 10:27–29 ESV)

> Surely goodness and mercy shall follow me
> all the days of my life,
> and I shall dwell in the house of the LORD forever.
> (Ps. 23:6 ESV)

Dear Father,

Thank you for adopting us into your family. Thank you for loving us and calling us your children. We are so excited about having a home with you forever! Thank you for creating the special animals we saw today. Please give them new owners who will love them and take good care of them. Watch over each one and keep them safe. Amen!

5

You're All Wet

☞ Grab

» Water balloons
» Two buckets or other large
   containers

» Towels
» Paper and pencils

Go

Get dressed in clothing you can get soaked in. Work together to fill up the water balloons. Place half of them in each of the two buckets.

Take your buckets of balloons to an open area outdoors. Stand a few feet apart and gently toss a water balloon back and forth. Back up a step and continue tossing the balloon. Gradually increase your distance apart and see how long you can make each balloon last as you play catch. Continue until all the water balloons have burst, or until it's just more fun to throw them *at* each other. (It doesn't hurt to have a couple of water guns on hand in case you run out of ammo!)

Once you've dried off for the day, take some time to talk about the following ideas together.

Grow

It takes a gentle hand to keep the balloon in one piece, doesn't it? Did you have to be patient with each other when you missed a catch or dropped one? One thing is for sure—you can't put a water balloon back together once it breaks.

That's a little bit like our feelings. We have to be careful with one another or we can really break each other's hearts. A thoughtless word, a sarcastic remark, a quick temper, a broken promise—these can create hurt feelings and a broken relationship. Read these verses together:

> Put on then, as God's chosen ones, holy and beloved, compassionate hearts, kindness, humility, meekness, and patience, bearing with one another and, if one has a complaint against another, forgiving each other; as the Lord has forgiven you, so you also must forgive. And above all these put on love, which binds everything together in perfect harmony. (Col. 3:12–14 ESV)

Take some time for each of you to write down just one thing you need to apologize for on a slip of paper. Have you broken any promises to each other? Have you lost your patience? Forgotten your manners? Today is the day to bring any hurts into the light and put the past behind you.

Give each other your slips of paper to read. Take your pencils and write "I forgive you" in big letters across the papers. Then tear up the papers and throw them away!

Dear Lord,

Thank you for showing us how we can live in peace together. You teach us how to be patient, forgiving, and loving. Thank you for giving us this time to make things right with each other. Just like we forgave each other today, you forgive us each and every day for every single sin. You give us clean hearts and second chances. Please grow our love for each other and for you. Amen!

6

That's Amore!

☞ Grab

» Pizza crust mix

» Jar of pizza sauce

» Shredded cheese

» Your favorite pizza toppings

Go

Set the table to create your own pizzeria—tablecloth, dishes, candles, and dinner music. Give your "restaurant" a name and have your daughter create a sign and/or menus with crayons and paper.

Make your way to the kitchen. Put on aprons to protect your clothes. Follow the package directions to prepare a pizza crust for each of you. Carefully spoon pizza sauce over the crusts and sprinkle on some shredded cheese. Add your favorite toppings and bake your pizzas in the oven until hot and bubbly. While they bake, have a little cleanup time—Mom will appreciate it!

When the pizzas are finished baking, enjoy your meal together.

Grow

There's nothing better than a pizza just the way you like it. I personally prefer a Chicago stuffed pizza with pepperoni and black olives. My girls prefer a hand-tossed pineapple and Canadian bacon pizza, and my son goes for barbecue chicken pizza every time.

Just like pizzas are made to order, God makes each of us exactly the way he had in mind. He gave each person their own unique talents, and has special plans for how he wants us to use our gifts and talents to serve him.

> For just as each of us has one body with many members, and these members do not all have the same function, so in Christ we, though many, form one body, and each member belongs to all the others. We have different gifts, according to the grace given to each of us. (Rom. 12:4–6)

For we are God's handiwork, created in Christ Jesus to do good works, which God prepared in advance for us to do. (Eph. 2:10)

Won't it be exciting to see what God has in store for you and me?

Picture your kids at school tomorrow. Or on some other field of battle. Envision them attending college, launching a career, or starting a family. What can you do today to help them succeed tomorrow?

Jay Payleitner, *52 Things Kids Need from a Dad*

Dear God,

Thank you for giving each of us our own special gifts and talents. Please teach us how to use them for you. Help us to be humble about our gifts, understanding that everything we do depends on your help and strength. Teach us to appreciate the talents we see in others without being jealous. Help us to see how amazing you are by the special gifts we see in others. We are so thankful for the church you have made, and the way you love us through our brothers and sisters in Christ. Amen!

7

Lights, Camera, Action!

☞ Grab

» *Goldilocks and the Three Bears* story book
» Video-capable camera or Smartphone
» Three stuffed bears

» Blonde-haired doll
» Dishes
» Doll chairs and beds—be creative!

Go

Are you ready for some movie-making magic? Create the story of *Goldilocks and the Three Bears*, one scene at a time, by arranging the toys and other items on a tabletop "set." Have your daughter decide which of you will narrate the story and who will be the cameraman that films the scenes. Your daughter may even want to play the part of Goldilocks herself! Load your completed film onto a computer. If you like, use your system's software to add music and special effects. Pop some popcorn and have fun watching your movie premiere!

> **Dad to Dad**
>
> *If your daughter is like mine, she'll want to post her video on YouTube within minutes! Other girls may want to pass on the movie-making and create a stage play instead. Have a great time acting out the story together using the doll and stuffed animals.*

⚜ Grow

We don't know much about Goldilocks other than her bad habit of breaking into people's houses! We know more about the bears, who appreciate a healthy diet and exercise and like to do everything as a family. We even know their furniture preferences. What is your family known for? Are you the biggest sports fans? The most musical? The ones who help out their neighbors? The ones with the brightest Christmas light display on the block?

The Bible has a lot to say about what God's people are to be known for. Consider what Jesus says in John 13:34–35:

> A new command I give you: Love one another. As I have loved you, so you must love one another. By this everyone will know that you are my disciples, if you love one another.

How will we be known as followers of Christ? By our love for each other! Even in your time together today, the caring and attention you are giving each other is your way of sharing the love of God. How amazing that caring for each other connects us with the heart of God himself.

Dear Father,

Thank you for giving us a new identity as your children. Please give us loving hearts so that the world sees you when it sees us. We want to care for each other in a way that stands out, just like your love for us is too big to miss! Please use us to be a light in the darkness. Amen!

8

Play with Your Food

Grab

- Potato peeler
- Knife and cutting board
- Carrots, cucumbers, celery, mushrooms, and peppers
- Cherry tomatoes
- Cheese slices
- Olives, nuts, and raisins
- Potato chips and pretzel sticks
- Vegetable dip
- Bowls
- Large tray or plates

Go

Wash your hands thoroughly. Use the potato peeler to cut long strips of carrots and cucumbers. Slice the vegetables and cheese into various sizes. Have your daughter place the vegetables, chips, pretzels, and other snacks in bowls. On your tray or empty plates, arrange the different pieces of food to make silly faces, animals, vehicles, flowers, etc. When you've had lots of fun "playing with your food," enjoy eating it up with the vegetable dip.

Dad to Dad

While it's an important part of the date to work together, keep your daughter's safety in mind when using knives and other kitchen tools.

Grow

What kinds of crazy food art ended up on your plates? Faces with carrot-strip hair, mushroom ears, and a smile made of olives? Your creations were inevitably funny—and tasty too.

Just like it's fun for you to watch your daughter's imagination go wild, thinking about God's creation of the world can blow your mind. Our planet is colorful and complex, but he made it all simply by his Word!

> For in him all things were created: things in heaven and on earth, visible and invisible, whether thrones or powers or rulers or authorities; all things have been created through him and for him. (Col. 1:16)

The Lord has plans for your daughter's own creativity. The imagination she possesses is part of God's fingerprint—she is made in his image. Will she create a loving home of her own someday? Perhaps she will create works of art or music, share her thoughts through the written word, or weave ideas and plans together to bless her community, church, and workplace.

Make a list together of all the ways your daughter has used her creativity recently. Did she draw a picture, rearrange her room, or write a clever poem? Did she invent an imaginary world for her stuffed animals to live in? Get excited about her efforts and consider how you can encourage her originality even more.

Dear Lord,

Thank you for giving us an imagination. Thank you, too, for your amazing creativity in making this world for us to live in. We love the way we can see you in what you have made—the sun, moon, and stars, the trees and mountains, and the people that we love. Amen.

9

Bubble Trouble

☞ Grab

» ½ cup of liquid dish soap
» 4 cups of bottled or distilled water
» 2 tablespoons of glycerin or light corn syrup

» Plastic cups
» Wire coat hanger
» Plastic straws
» Rubber bands
» Large jar or container

Go

In a large jar or container, gently mix together the dish soap, water, and glycerin or corn syrup. Let the bubble solution stand for several hours—your bubbles will last longer.

Have fun creating bubble-blowing tools together. Cut the bottom from plastic cups to make rings. Bend a wire coat hanger to make a large circle. (For safety, you may wish to wrap the ends of the wire with duct tape.) Cluster several straws together and wrap them with rubber bands to hold them together. Let your daughter gather a variety of items such as slotted spoons, the plastic rings that hold soda cans together, or plastic funnels.

Put on some play clothes and head outdoors to create bubble mania! See how many tiny bubbles you can make at one time. Or create the largest, longest-lasting bubble you possibly can. Experiment with catching bubbles with wet hands or with soft gloves on, or try to pass them back and forth between you. Blow as many bubbles as you can at once, and try to pop them all in the air before they reach the ground.

> **Dad to Dad**
>
> *Don't stress about spilling the bubble solution or getting sticky—you can hose yourselves off later!*

Grow

Isn't it interesting that despite the variety of tools you used to create the bubbles, each one came out in exactly the same shape? No matter the method, you get clear, shiny spheres every time.

The Word of God says the same thing about God's people: true faith looks the same in all of us despite our individuality. First John 4:7 says, "Beloved, let us love one another, for love is from God, and whoever loves has been born of God and knows God" (ESV). All of God's true children show *love*.

Tell your daughter how you have observed her love for you and others through her words and behavior this past week. Share a memory of when you felt her love through a gift or other special expression. Where have you seen her concern and compassion for others? Share these observations with your daughter and express how beautiful her loving heart is to you. And of course, end your time together with an "I love you" of your own.

Dear loving Father,

Thank you for loving us no matter what. Help us to never doubt how high and wide and deep your love for us really is. Please give us loving hearts for everyone around us every day. Thank you for my daughter's caring heart—you have blessed me through her in a thousand ways. Amen.

10

A Walk in the Night

☛ Grab

» Flashlight
» Blanket

» Thermos of hot
   cocoa

Go

Once it is fully dark outside, place your blanket and hot cocoa in a backpack. Make your way to a safe outdoor location together, such as a friend's rural property, your church's grounds, or your own backyard. When you arrive, have your daughter turn on the flashlight. Grab the backpack and begin your "Walk in the Night." Make your way to a good spot to spread your blanket and sit together. Encourage your daughter to walk slowly and hold your hand so she doesn't trip and fall.

Move quietly so you can listen to the sounds around you. Do you hear any owls or other animals? Is the wind moving through the tree branches? Is there a creek or river close by with water rushing over the rocks? Do you hear cars driving in the distance?

Enjoy drinking the hot cocoa and talking through some of the questions and ideas below.

ᛘ Grow

Ask your daughter these questions:

» Was it scary walking in the dark with only a flashlight to show the way?

» What would have happened if we had tried to walk without it?

» What would it feel like to be outdoors at night alone instead of together?

» Are there sights or sounds we noticed around us tonight that we might have missed if it was daytime?

Did holding her daddy's hand give your daughter confidence as you went outdoors after dark? Our Father God is always ready to hold our hand, too, as we make our way through life. As the psalmist says, "Your hand shall lead me, and your right hand shall hold me" (Ps. 139:10 ESV).

Psalm 27:1 says, "The LORD is my light and my salvation; whom shall I fear?" When we feel like we're in the dark because of troubles we're going through, we don't have to be afraid because God shows the way and gives us courage.

The Bible also says, "Your word is a lamp to my feet and a light to my path" (Ps. 119:105 ESV). Sometimes we don't know what to do. We're confused, sad, or don't understand why things are happening to us. In times like that we can read the Word of God and find help and wisdom to get through it.

Dear Lord,

Thank you for being our light in the darkness. Help us to trust you and not be afraid even when we are going through something difficult. Teach us your Word so we have the light of truth in every situation. Thank you for my daughter and this beautiful evening we were able to enjoy together. We love you! Amen.

11

Treasure Hunt

☞ Grab

» Twenty index cards
» Treat or small gift for your daughter

» Pen
» Gift bag or wrapping paper

Go

Wrap the treat or gift to make it a special surprise for your daughter. Number the index cards from 1 to 20. Hide card number 20 with the treat or small gift in a clever hiding place. On the back of card number 19, write a clue about the location of card number 20. Hide card number 19, and write a clue about its location on card number 18. Continue hiding the cards and writing clues about their hiding places until cards 2 through 20 are hidden. Save card 1 to give your daughter at the beginning of the game.

> **Dad to Dad**
>
> *Keep your daughter's reading level and age in mind. A young, beginning reader could read clues such as "in a cup" or "in the tub." An older daughter's clues can be more complex, such as "where things tumble" (in the dryer), "where Dad finds strength to face the day" (the coffee pot), or "where we see the future" (the calendar).*

Give card 1 to your daughter. Tag along with her as she works her way through the clues. Feel free to give little hints if she gets stuck—the game should be challenging enough to be fun but not so hard that she gets frustrated. Praise her when she figures out a really tricky clue. Celebrate with her when she finds the special gift at the end!

🌱 Grow

Did your daughter think the hiding places were funny and unexpected? At any point in the search, did she get tired or confused? Was it fun watching her "aha!" moments when she figured out the harder clues?

> One of life's greatest mysteries is how the boy who wasn't good enough to marry your daughter can be the father of the smartest grandchild in the world.
>
> Author Unknown

The one thing about a treasure hunt is that it takes persistence to make it to the prize at the end. We should have that same determination when it comes to finding wisdom and deepening our knowledge of God.

In Proverbs 2:3–5, Solomon encourages his child to:

> call out for insight
> and cry aloud for understanding,
> and if you look for it as for silver
> and search for it as for hidden treasure,
> then you will understand the fear of the LORD
> and find the knowledge of God.

Use the "clues" in Scripture, in the teaching you find at church, and in your prayer time to eagerly hunt for wisdom. The most exciting prize we will ever receive is finding the truth of who God is!

Dear God,

Help us to search for wisdom as a great treasure. We want to find wisdom so we can know you better and worship you. Teach us your truth through your Word so we will trust you more as we follow you. Amen!

12

Wash Your Wheels

☞ Grab

» Bucket
» Mild dish detergent or car wash
  solution

» Garden hose
» Soft brush or rags
» Glass cleaner

Go

Dress in clothing you can get soaked in. Fill a bucket with detergent and water from the hose. Work together to scrub your car clean on the outside and polish the windows on the inside. Let your daughter use the hose to spray off the soap (and you, of course!). If you're feeling really ambitious, take the floor mats out and let her vacuum them clean. Praise her for a job well done.

> **Dad to Dad**
>
> *Guys, this is not the time to be a perfectionist! She may miss a spot or two, and her young arms aren't strong enough to scrub off the tough stuff. This also isn't the time to lecture her about the crumbs and items she has cluttered the car with. Just have fun getting wet and let the professionals detail the vehicle more thoroughly next time.*

✴ Grow

Talk about why your car was so dirty. Is the mud on the flaps from the last rainy day you had? Are the bugs on the windshield from your recent drive in the country? Our vehicles lose their shine as they travel through the mud and muck of the world around us.

The same is true for our hearts sometimes. It can be hard to keep a pure heart when the sin of the world is surrounding us. Talk about the following verses, and be encouraged!

> Finally, brothers and sisters, whatever is true, whatever is noble, whatever is right, whatever is pure, whatever is lovely, whatever is admirable—if anything is excellent or praiseworthy—think about such things. (Phil. 4:8)

> If we confess our sins, he is faithful and just and will forgive us our sins and purify us from all unrighteousness. (1 John 1:9)

> Grace and peace to you from God our Father and the Lord Jesus Christ, who gave himself for our sins to rescue us from the present evil age, according to the will of our God and Father. (Gal. 1:3–4)

Dear Father,

Thank you for forgiving us of all our sins and giving us clean hearts. We pray that you would make us holy, just like you are holy. Protect us from loving the world more than we love you. We want to look like Jesus! Amen.

13

Up in the Air

☞ Grab

» Several large balloons   » Tape
» Crepe paper streamers or yarn » Scissors

Go

Take a deep breath, and blow up several balloons with your daughter. In a room with some open space, tape one end of a crepe paper streamer or piece of yarn to the wall a few feet up from the floor. Stretch the streamer across the middle of the room and tape the other end to the opposite wall.

Standing on opposite sides of the streamer "net," begin hitting a balloon back and forth. Try not to let the balloon touch the ground. Count how many times you can "volley" before the balloon gets away from you. For a challenge, add in a second balloon and see if you can keep both balloons going over the streamer at the same time.

Gather your balloons together near a bare wall. Rub the balloons on your clothing and hair to create static electricity. See how many electrified balloons you can get to stick to the wall at the same time!

Sit on the floor and see if you can keep a balloon in the air by using only your feet to keep it from touching the ground. Try the same thing standing and using only your head and your elbows!

When you're finished with balloon games for the day, take your scissors and cut a small slit near the knot in each balloon. Let the balloons go and see how far they will fly before they run out of air.

Grow

You can't play with a balloon if it's empty, can you? Well, you could try, but you'd be bored in a hurry! It's the air inside a balloon that fills it up so it can float and bounce.

We are empty and need to be filled up too. We need to be filled with the Holy Spirit so we can live like Jesus in the world. Galatians 5:22–23 tells us, "The fruit of the Spirit is love, joy, peace, forbearance, kindness, goodness, faithfulness, gentleness and self-control."

How are these "fruits" growing in you? Take turns describing how you have lately seen each fruit in action in each other.

Dear God,

Thank you for the gift of the Holy Spirit that helps us to be like Jesus. Please grow our love, joy, and peace so the world can see you in us. Teach us to be kind, good, and faithful to our families and friends. May we be gentle and self-controlled even when we're frustrated or having a hard day. Thank you that we don't have to make ourselves better—you give us your Spirit to change us from the inside out. We love you! Amen.

14

Catch a Falling Star

☞ Grab

» Your news report, indicating the optimum nights for watching a summer meteor shower

» Blankets or sleeping bags
» Cold drinks and snacks

Go

Travel to a park or rural location where street lights are at a minimum. Meteors are best viewed in as dark a setting as possible. Find an open area with a clear view of the sky to spread out your blankets. Get comfortable!

Relax and keep your eyes on the skies above. Enjoy the excitement with your daughter of spotting the beautiful "shooting stars" as they appear. If the timing is right you may be treated to quite a show, so keep count of how many you see.

Enjoy some cold drinks and snacks as you talk about Abraham's night of watching the stars with God.

> **Dad to Dad**
>
> *This is a wonderful experience, but keep safety in mind as you choose your outdoor location. A public park may not be as safe as sharing a friend's backyard. A local planetarium may offer suggestions for good viewing sites.*

🌱 Grow

Genesis 15 tells the story of how, on one starry night, the Lord God brought Abraham out to look at the sky with him. He challenged Abraham to count the stars if he was able. God then made an amazing promise to Abraham: his family would one day number as many as the stars in the night sky.

That was an unbelievable promise for a man who didn't even have a single child! In fact, he and his wife were so old that having children was impossible. Yet even though it seemed too miraculous to believe, Abraham trusted God. As the story unfolds in Scripture, we see that God kept his promise and created a whole nation of people from Abraham's family. The most wonderful part of the story is that our Savior, Jesus Christ, was born into the world as a member of that family.

God promises us that if we put our trust in Jesus we are adopted into his family. Whenever we look at the stars we can remember God's plan for Abraham—and for us—to belong to the family of God forever.

Dear Father,

Thank you for your promises and that nothing is impossible for you. We are so thankful that just as you made Abraham and his children a part of your family, you have invited us to be your children too. Thank you that every time we look at the stars in the sky, we can remember that we are part of your forever family. Amen!

15

Time Capsule

☞ Grab

» Plastic storage container with a lid
» Plastic storage bags
» Current newspaper, magazine, and clothing catalog
» Samples of your daughter's recent artwork
» Photographs of family and friends

» Various mementos such as award ribbons, stickers, special homework assignments, small toys, favorite Bible verses, etc.
» Clean packaging from your daughter's favorite snacks

Go

Begin packing the container together. Place photographs and paper items in plastic storage bags before packing them away. Talk about how the headlines in the newspaper and the fashions in the catalog will probably seem like "old news" after a short amount of time. Ask her if she thinks the homework she's saving will seem as challenging in the future as it was for her at the time. Does she think the snacks she prefers now will still be her favorites when she's older?

Find a corner of the yard where the container can be buried. Take care to avoid tree roots and any area where pipes or electrical wires could be under the soil. Let your daughter help dig a hole to bury the container.

Plan a date to dig it up again! One year or two years from now? Or does your daughter wish to add a few items to the container each year? Make a plan and put it on the calendar as a reminder.

〰 Grow

Nobody knows more than a parent how time can fly. Wasn't your daughter an infant, say, *yesterday*? You've seen her change and grow from year to year. A time capsule is a wonderful way to make a "snapshot" of who she is right at this moment in time.

> A daughter may outgrow your lap, but she will never outgrow your heart.
>
> Author Unknown

Ask your daughter these questions:

» What can you do now that you couldn't do when you were two years old?

» What can you do now that was hard when you were five?

» What do you think you will be able to do when you're seventeen that you can't do now? What about when you're twenty? Forty?

God is well aware of how each of us grows and changes year by year. In fact, he promises to help us grow more like Jesus until we see him face-to-face in heaven. It's encouraging to know that he doesn't give up on us even when we are slow learners, but keeps on working in us every single day.

Hebrews 13:21 says God will "equip you with everything good that you may do his will, working in us that which is pleasing in his sight, through Jesus Christ" (ESV).

It's encouraging to know that "He has made everything beautiful in its time" (Eccles. 3:11). He's doing a wonderful work in us, right on time!

Dear Lord,

Thank you for working in us to make us more like Jesus. Thank you for being patient with us even when we're slow to learn and grow. Thank you, too, that we don't have to work hard to make ourselves perfect because you are the one who gives us a new heart and mind. You are so good to us! Amen.

16

Shadow Fun

☛ Grab

» Desk lamp or bright flashlight   » Thick paper, scissors
» Bare wall   » Assorted household items

Go

Once it is fully dark for the evening, place the desk lamp or flashlight so that it shines on a bare wall. Use your imaginations to make shadow puppets with your hands or by cutting characters out of paper. Team up to act out a fairy tale with your shadow puppets, or let your daughter create a story and perform it for you.

See if you can make your shadows overlap on the wall. Can her shadow fit inside of yours? See if your shadows can shake hands without your hands actually touching. By tilting or moving the light, can you make your shadows change size and shape? Can you pose to make life-sized shadows of the letters of the alphabet?

Play "guess the shadow" by taking turns holding up various items in front of the light. Can you tell if it's a shadow of a toothbrush? A candle? Eyeglasses? A teapot? A plant? See how tricky you can make it for each other!

Tape a piece of black paper to the wall and have your daughter stand in front of it. Position her so that she's standing sideways with the shadow of her profile centered on the paper. Take a white crayon or chalk and carefully trace the outline of her profile on the paper. Remove the paper from the wall, cut around the outline, and paste it to a piece of white or colored paper. Write her name and the date on the back and save the special keepsake you've created.

ꙮ Grow

A shadow is formed when someone or something is blocking the light. It's interesting how a small object can cast a huge shadow. Has your daughter ever been frightened of a shadow at night that was really something small and harmless?

Sometimes we get spooked by "shadows" when problems seem bigger than they really are. We can forget to take our troubles to God, who can bring them down to size by his promises to love and care for us.

Let's remember God's instruction to "Humble yourselves, therefore, under God's mighty hand, that he may lift you up in due time. Cast all your anxiety on him because he cares for you" (1 Pet. 5:6–7).

Dear Father,

Thank you for your great love for us. You care about every one of our worries and troubles. Thank you for your promise to watch over us and get us through hard times. Give us courage to face the things that make us afraid. Grow our faith in you so that we can have peace in our hearts no matter what "shadows" we face. Amen.

17

Parachutes

☞ Grab

» Two plastic grocery or trash bags
» String, cut into eight eighteen-inch pieces

» Two rubber bands
» Two small plastic animals or dolls

Go

Let's make parachutes! Cut a square from each plastic bag, about a foot or so across. Cut a small hole into each corner of your squares. Tie a length of string to each of the corners of the bag. Gather the ends of the strings and knot them together. Use a rubber band to attach a small plastic toy to the knotted part of the string.

Without tangling the strings, carefully fold the parachute into a small bundle. Lightly wrap the string and toy around it. Toss your parachute into the air, and as the string unwinds the parachute will open and float to the ground.

> **Dad to Dad**
> *Make sure safety comes first with this date! Even though it's fun to drop parachutes from a high point, do not allow your daughter to lean out over a railing or windowsill or climb where there is any danger of falling.*

❦ Grow

You would never jump out of an airplane without a parachute! You would put your trust in that chute in your pack to keep you from harm as you fell toward the earth. That's just like life—we would not want to face the future and all of its unknowns without being under the watchful care of God.

> Cast your cares on the LORD and he will sustain you;
> he will never let the righteous be shaken. (Ps. 55:22)

> The LORD makes firm the steps,
> of the one who delights in him;
> though he may stumble, he will not fall,
> for the LORD upholds him with his hand. (Ps. 37:23–24)

God is ready and able to help us in any situation. Talk to him about everything going on in your life today—he wants to share his strength and love with you as you lean on him.

Dear Father,

Thank you for being there for us every single day. Thank you for your promise to keep us from falling. With you we can keep on going even when things are difficult. Teach us to depend on you—with you we'll never fall! Amen.

18

Be a Blessing to Mom

☞ Grab

» Mom's favorite juice, coffee, or tea
» Muffins or bagels

» Flower in a vase
» Paper and markers or crayons

Go

Choose a morning and dedicate it to blessing Mom with your daughter. Get up together early in the morning and make Mom a special card. List the things that you love about her and thank her for all she does for your family.

Prepare Mom's favorite juice, coffee, or tea, and put together a simple breakfast for her. Place the breakfast, card, and flower on a tray and treat her to breakfast in bed.

After breakfast, spend some time with your daughter serving Mom in creative ways. Take a trash bag and clean out her car. Take her shopping list and run errands for her so she can relax. Shop for a thoughtful gift, like a flower to plant in the yard, a set of scented bath items, a pretty pen or calendar for her purse, or a bag of freshly ground gourmet coffee. Maybe there's a honey-do project you've been putting off for a while that your daughter could help you with.

However you spend your time, keep Mom in the center of your thoughts and conversation. Use the time to talk about why Mom is special to each of you. Brainstorm together about ways you can be a blessing to her every single day.

Dad to Dad

Perhaps Mom isn't living with you at this time. If this is due to a divorce or separation, it is a tremendous benefit to your daughter to see the way you honor her mother. We love like Christ when we serve others selflessly without expecting anything in return.

If you are parenting alone for other reasons, choose another woman who is significant in your daughter's life whom you can serve together. A teacher, a friend, or a close relative will appreciate your thanks for her part in caring for your daughter.

𝄞 Grow

A mother's life centers around the well-being of her family. She juggles countless details to keep the household running and make sure each person in the family is cared for. Sometimes she runs out of time or energy to take care of herself. Recognizing her loving efforts and taking the time to lighten her load, even for one day, means so much to a busy mom!

Read Proverbs 31:10–31 with your daughter. Take note of the ways that Mom compares to the wife and mother in the passage. Does she get up early to make school lunches? Does she juggle a career on top of managing the household? Does she encourage each of you with her words? Today you took the time to "arise and call her blessed" (v. 28)!

Dear Lord,

Thank you for the gift of Mom! She loves us so much, in so many ways. We see your love for us through her words and the way she takes care of us. Please teach us how to encourage her each day. Help us to be faithful to care for her just like she is always there for us. Bless her in every way. Amen!

19

Silly Sock Day

☞ Grab

» Money
» Car keys
» Small notebook and pencil

Go

Make your way to a mall or shopping center. Your goal: get the silliest, wackiest pair of socks for each of you that you can find! Take your time browsing through the stores. Let your daughter make note of the wildest pair of socks in each store, so at the end of your browsing you can go back to purchase your favorites.

Once you've made your purchases, enjoy a snack at the food court.

Put on your silly socks at home. They can be your secret sign to each other. Whenever you see your daughter's socks or she sees yours, it means "I'm crazy about you!"

〰 Grow

Sometimes life is just too serious. Our to-do lists never end, the phone doesn't stop ringing, and the nightly reports bring a daily dose of bad news. We need a break from time to time to leave our worries behind and get silly together.

Ecclesiastes 3:1–4 reminds us that:

There is a time for everything, and a season for every activity under the heavens:
> a time to be born and a time to die,
> a time to plant and a time to uproot,
> a time to kill and a time to heal,
> a time to tear down and a time to build,
> a time to weep and a time to laugh,
> a time to mourn and a time to dance.

Today was your time to laugh! Whenever you see your socks in the drawer or on your feet, let them be a reminder to lighten up more often and enjoy the funny side of life together.

Dear God,

You give us so many reasons to smile—especially by the way you put my daughter and I together. Please let our silly socks be a reminder of your gift of laughter every time we wear them. Thank you for giving me such a fun girl to spend time with. Amen!

20

Picnic at the Park

☞ Grab

» Small cooler
» Sandwich fixings
» Chips, cookies, etc.
» Fruit

» Water bottles or juice boxes
» Outdoor blanket or sleeping bag
» Ball

Go

Work together in the kitchen to prepare a picnic lunch. Your daughter can help make the sandwiches and fill plastic bags with chips. She can wash fruit and help pack the cooler. Praise her for pitching in to help.

Choose a park with a playground to visit together. Have fun walking or biking to the park, or have fun driving in the car with the radio turned up loud!

Have a blast playing together at the park—push her on the swings, chase her around the equipment, and tickle her when she reaches the bottom of the slide. Play tag and hide-and-seek, and play catch with the ball. The main idea is to *play*!

When you're ready for a break, spread out the blanket and enjoy your picnic lunch. Savor this time with your daughter and feel like a kid again!

Dad to Dad

Sometimes it's hard to clear your mind of all your many responsibilities. There are always issues at work to think about and things needing repair

---

56

at home. Challenge yourself to be fully present with your daughter today. Leave your cell phone and iPod in the car. Try to put your cares aside for a little while so she can enjoy having her daddy's undivided attention. It will be a gift to both of you!

🌱 Grow

Proverbs 17:22 says that "a cheerful heart is good medicine." Hopefully playing together today was a chance to lighten your heart and "cure" you of any negativity and stress you've been carrying. Perhaps it also brought some healing between you and your daughter. Have the worries of life been distracting you from your relationship lately? Have the stresses at work affected your patience with her? May today be a step toward rebuilding the bridge between you.

Dear Lord,

Thank you for being the perfect Father who always has time to help and spend time with his children. Thank you for wanting to be close to us even when we fail to reach out to you. Thanks for giving me the greatest gift in the world—the chance to be the dad of this amazing girl. Help us to be close and to really stick together even when our days are so busy. We're thankful for the chance to play today. You knew what we needed! We love you. Amen.

21

Backyard Campout

☞ Grab

» Tent and sleeping bags
» Marshmallows, graham crackers, chocolate bars

» Fire bowl or pit, wood
» Flashlights
» Bedtime stories

Go

While it's still daylight, work together with your daughter to set up the tent. Let her help with hammering in the tent stakes and zipping up the flaps. When it's nearly dark, work together to build a fire (keeping safety in mind!). Roast marshmallows and make sticky, yummy s'mores.

When you're ready to settle in for the night, teach your daughter fire safety by carefully covering or extinguishing your campfire. Get comfortable in your sleeping bags (or as comfortable as possible!). Use your flashlight as a reading light to enjoy bedtime stories together. Let your daughter say her bedtime prayers with you.

After "lights out," talk together about the following ideas.

☿ Grow

A campfire is one of the most important elements of a campout. It gives light, warmth, and a means of making the best treat ever— s'mores! Without a fire, camping would be a pretty sorry experience.

Isn't it interesting how fire can be so beautiful and useful, yet so dangerous at the same time? If we use fire correctly it's a blessing, and if we handle it wrong it can cause serious pain and destruction.

James talks about how our tongue is like a fire, too. Our words can be a blessing or cause great harm.

> In the same way the tongue is a small part of the body, but it can brag about doing important things. A large forest can be set on fire by a little flame. (James 3:5 GW)

> A truly rich man is one whose children run into his arms when his hands are empty.
>
> **Author Unknown**

Verses 9–10 go on to say,

> With our tongues we praise our Lord and Father. Yet, with the same tongues we curse people, who were created in God's likeness. Praise and curses come from the same mouth. My brothers and sisters, this should not happen! (GW)

The Lord wants us to use our words to bless each other, just like your campfire gives wonderful warmth and light on a dark night. Our speech should be kind, honest, and build each other up. We shouldn't use our words to gossip or "burn" each other with sarcasm and put-downs. Talk to God together about your words right now.

Dear God,

Thank you for giving us the gift of words. We love being able to talk to each other and to you. Please help us keep control over what we say. Forgive us for the times we have used our words to lie, make fun of someone, criticize, complain, or gossip. Give us a new start with how we speak—honestly, gently, and lovingly like Jesus. Thank you! Amen.

22

A Beautiful Day
in the Neighborhood

☛ Grab

» Bag of chocolate chips
» Baking utensils and ingredients
» Waxed paper
» Paper lunch sacks

» Stickers and markers
» Paper hole punch
» Scissors and curling ribbon

Go

Wash your hands and prepare to bake cookies together. Follow the cookie recipe on the bag of chocolate chips to bake several dozen cookies. Allow your daughter to help with the baking as much as possible. Let her crack the eggs (never mind the mess), pour the ingredients into the bowl, and help use the mixer. Keep safety in mind as you handle the oven and hot baking pans.

While the cookies are cooling, put away the baking ingredients and clean up the kitchen together. Let your daughter put on dish gloves and help wash the dishes. After things are straightened up, sit with your daughter while she decorates several paper lunch sacks. Talk together about the neighbors that will be receiving each bag of cookies. This would be a good opportunity to talk about manners, such as introducing yourself politely and saying, "Have a nice day."

Wrap several cookies in waxed paper and place them in one of the paper sacks. Fold the sack closed, punch holes through the top, and run ribbon through the holes to tie it shut. Show your daughter how to curl the ribbon with the edge of the scissors. Repeat this until each sack is filled and ready to deliver.

Walk around your neighborhood with your daughter. Let her ring the doorbells and encourage her to say hello and introduce herself to neighbors you might not know. Give the cookies to your neighbors and wish them a nice day.

When you get home, take some time to talk about the following verses and pray for the special people in your neighborhood.

🌱 Grow

It's a familiar verse—"You shall love your neighbor as yourself" (Matt. 19:19 ESV). But why should we concern ourselves with caring for the people around us? They probably don't take much notice of us, either.

The reason is that when we show love to others, we are showing the love of Christ. If we belong to God, then we are to "be imitators of God, as beloved children. And walk in love, as Christ loved us and gave himself up for us, a fragrant offering and sacrifice to God" (Eph. 5:1–2 ESV).

Dear Lord,

Please allow our neighbors to see you through the way we love and care for them. If any of our neighbors don't know you as their Savior, please lead them to salvation. Please help us to show your love to each and every neighbor so that your light shines. Give us chances to help and serve our neighbors so we can be "imitators of God" as we "walk in love." Amen!

23

Animal Pancakes

☞ Grab

» Pancake mix
» Empty ketchup bottle
» Chocolate chips

Go

Team up with your daughter to prepare pancake batter using the recipe on the container of pancake mix. Heat a skillet to medium heat on the stove. Fill an empty ketchup bottle with pancake batter and place the cap on top. Use the bottle to squeeze batter onto your hot skillet in the shape of various animals. A larger circle of batter with two circles at the top for ears makes a fun mouse or bear. Try various combinations of ovals and circles to make different animals, or spell out the letters of your daughter's name. Let her choose an animal for you to attempt, and if it doesn't turn out well it can be an "alien"!

Let your daughter use chocolate chips to create faces on her animal pancakes. Pour on some syrup and enjoy breakfast together.

🌾 Grow

The animal pancake that ended up on your plate may not have matched the original idea you had in mind. Creating a recognizable creature from liquid batter is a challenge! It takes a combination of the right temperature, just the right consistency of batter, and the dexterity of the cook to get the perfect pancake. (You should see my attempts at making pancake-batter penguins!)

God had everything he needed when it came to creating people—he had power and perfection! It's amazing that he had us in mind before he even created the world.

> I praise you because I am fearfully and wonderfully made;
> your works are wonderful,
> I know that full well.
> My frame was not hidden from you
> when I was made in the secret place,
> when I was woven together in the depths of the earth.
> Your eyes saw my unformed body;
> all the days ordained for me were written in your book
> before one of them came to be. (Ps. 139:14–16)

God imagined us, created us, led us to salvation, and has a future planned for us as well. Praise him!

Dear God,

> *Thank you for being our creator. It's so exciting to know that we are not an accident—you love us so much that you planned every detail of who we are and what our future holds. Please help us live for you, "holy and blameless" until we see you face-to-face. Amen!*

24

One, Two, Three, Go!

☞ Grab

» Money
» Car keys
» Bible

Go

Tell your daughter you're on a quest to find three things: something fun, something pretty, and something sweet.

Hop in the car and begin making your way to the nearest toy store. Use your drive time to talk about how much fun your daughter is. Reminisce about the goofy, silly memories you have of times together. Tell her about moments from her younger days that still bring a smile when you think about them.

When you arrive at the toy store, it's time to look for something fun! Set a spending limit and let your daughter search through the store for an inexpensive game or toy.

Hit the road again and head for a drugstore or "girly" store like Claire's or Justice. (From my own personal research, no father has yet died from overexposure to feminine retail outlets!) Use your time in the car to talk about how beautiful your daughter is. Ask her what she likes best about herself, and talk about how beauty counts just as much on the inside. Share with your daughter what you find beautiful about her mother too. Once you reach the drugstore, let your daughter choose something that makes her feel pretty—some hair clips, nail polish, lip gloss, or inexpensive jewelry.

Finally, begin making your way to a favorite restaurant for a special dessert. As you drive, talk about how sweet your daughter is to you. Point out some of her recent sweet comments, thoughtful moments, and the ways she has been kind to her family, friends, or even strangers. At the restaurant enjoy your "sweets" and talk about the following ideas together.

Grow

Was it fun finding something fun, something pretty, and something sweet? Hopefully it's clear by this point in your date that your daughter is all of those things to you.

Read Psalm 127:3–5 together:

> Children are an inheritance from the LORD.
> They are a reward from him.
> The children born to a man when he is young are like ar-
> rows in the hand of a warrior.
> Blessed is the man who has filled his quiver with them.
> (GW)

Your daughter is God's gift and reward to you! God calls her your inheritance and blessing. Could anything be better?

Dear Lord,

Thank you for the gift of my daughter. I love her fun personality, her beauty inside and out, and her sweetness to me and our family. Thank you for this time to enjoy with her. She is the most amazing blessing I could ever imagine. Amen!

25

Bowling

☛ Grab

- » Money
- » Car keys

Go

Check your local bowling alley's schedule for discount days or special events like neon bowling nights. Drive together to your local bowling alley. Rent your shoes, pick your ball, and have a great time bowling some games. Make sure to use the bumpers on the lane if your daughter is a beginning bowler. Celebrate your strikes and spares, and save your score sheet as a keepsake for your daughter.

Then sit down together with something to drink and talk about the following ideas together.

Grow

Did your daughter use the bumpers to keep her ball in the lane? Wouldn't it be great if grown-ups could use the bumpers, too?

The bumpers in the bowling lane are a lot like the boundaries a dad puts around his daughter. The rules and limits he puts over her are for her protection and well-being. They keep her from falling away from the right path or from getting into dangerous situations.

The bumpers probably made the bowling games a lot more fun for your daughter, compared to losing her ball in the gutter over and over. Sometimes it's hard for her to appreciate your rules that much, though! Read the following verses from Psalm 119 together:

> I will always obey your law,
> for ever and ever.
> I will walk about in freedom,
> for I have sought out your precepts. (vv. 44–45)

> Great peace have they who love your law,
> and nothing can make them stumble. (v. 165)

One way a daughter can obey the Lord is by obeying her earthly father. "Children, obey your parents in everything, for this pleases the Lord" (Col. 3:20). Limits and rules are given out of love, not to steal your daughter's joy. Being corrected isn't always fun. But we're given the promise that loving discipline "produces a harvest of righteousness and peace for those who have been trained by it" (Heb. 12:11). Aren't you glad that God loves us enough to correct us and keep us from going the wrong way?

Dear Father,

Thank you for your Word that teaches us how to live. We know that when we obey you, we find peace and freedom. Thank you for my daughter and for loving her so much. Please give me help in setting wise boundaries around her. I want to be kind and fair, and to help her be safe and stay on the right path. Please help my daughter receive my discipline and limits with a thankful heart. Help her to know that I want to obey you by the way I watch over her. Amen.

26

A Basket Full of Fun

☞ Grab

» Play clothes that can get dirty

» Sunscreen

» Bug spray

» Money

» Car keys

Go

Read through your newspaper classifieds to see which berries are in season and available to pick. Choose a u-pick berry farm and dress for the outdoors. Have a nice drive out in the country as you make your way to the farm.

Have a great time with your daughter picking buckets of fresh berries. Show your daughter how to pick the fruit carefully to avoid damaging the plants or crushing any berries. Challenge each other to see who can find the biggest, most perfect berries and who can fill their bucket first. Think ahead about how you can enjoy them at home—on ice cream, in a smoothie, in a pie, or on shortcake. Have a great time in the beautiful outdoors together!

✿ Grow

Is anything more delicious than fruit that's just been picked? Did you imagine all the wonderful things you (or Mom!) can make with the berries when you get home? Perhaps you can share some of your harvest with a neighbor or an elderly member of your church family.

Was the field or orchard picked clean or bursting with fruit? The Bible compares the world to a field ready to harvest. Luke 10:2 says that "the harvest is plentiful, but the workers are few. Ask the Lord of the harvest, therefore, to send out workers into his harvest field." Imagine how, for every berry you saw today, there is an individual in our world that is lost and in need of God's salvation.

Talk through these questions together:

> What can easily be missed is the importance of a father in a daughter's life. His kind words, respect, and affirmation of her beauty can help her see that her life is important and meaningful, which profoundly impacts her identity and character.
>
> Philip Carlson, MD,
> *Love Written in Stone*

» How can our family reach out to the lost in our community?

» In our country?

» In the world?

» What is our church doing right now to witness to the lost?

» How can we get involved in what our church is doing with missions?

Make a plan for just one thing you and your daughter will do this week to help spread the gospel. Make a donation to a missions organization, pray for a missionary, invite an unsaved family member or friend to a church event with you, or explore upcoming ministry opportunities with your church.

Just as the fruit you picked today was wonderful to discover, God rejoices over each person who finds new life in him.

Dear Lord,

Thank you for caring so much about every person in the world that is lost without you. May we have the same passion for reaching the world with the gospel that you do! Please give us the courage and the opportunity to tell others about the joy we have found in you. We are so excited that we are no longer lost, but found! Thank you for the incredible gift of salvation in Jesus. Amen!

27

A New "Do"

☞ Grab

» Camera
» Haircut money
» Car keys

Go

Before you head out to create your daughter's new hairstyle, use your camera to take a picture of her current look. Let her take a photo of you too. Then grab your wallet and camera and make your way to a salon.

At the salon, look through the books of hairstyles while you wait. Have fun looking at some of the outrageous styles on the various models in the books. Treat your daughter to a shampoo and a haircut. Ask the stylist to blow-dry your daughter's hair and perhaps curl, braid, or clip it up in a cute style. If the salon offers manicure services, go ahead and let your daughter choose a favorite color for her nails to be painted. When she's all finished "beautifying," take a picture of her great new look.

Wrap up your date with an ice cream cone and have fun comparing your daughter's before-and-after pictures.

> **Dad to Dad**
> *Check with Mom before making a drastic change to your daughter's hairstyle! Plan together with Mom and your daughter how short or different the new haircut will be. Make sure you know how to explain*

what you want to the stylist before you get there to avoid any unhappy surprises.

𝒲 Grow

Did you know that God knows each of us so well that "the very hairs of your head are all numbered" (Luke 12:7)? There is no detail about you or your daughter that escapes his notice. It's encouraging to know that he loves us completely and is watching over us every moment.

Thank him right now for making your daughter so beautiful and keeping her in his sight all the time.

Dear Father,

You did an amazing job when you made my daughter! Thank you for her pretty eyes, her awesome smile, and her beautiful hair. Thank you for watching over her all the time—it means so much to me that you are caring for her and protecting her even when I can't be there. Thanks for giving us this time together today. Amen!

10 Great Daddy-Daughter Songs

Cinderella by Steven Curtis Chapman
Butterfly Kisses by Bob Carlisle
Fathers and Daughters by Paul Simon
Dancin' on Daddy's Shoes by Leon Redbone
Stealing Cinderella by Chuck Wicks

I Hope You Dance by Lee Ann Womack or Ronan Keating
Do I Make You Proud by Taylor Hicks
Daddy's Little Girl by Kippi Brannon
My Little Girl by Tim McGraw
I Loved Her First by Heartland

Dad to Dad

For a special gift, burn a CD of these or other great daddy-daughter songs. You can listen to them in the car on your dates or play them in her room when you tuck her in at night.

28

Ice Skating

☛ Grab

» Warm, comfortable clothes
» Ice skates (or money for skate rental)

Go

Gather up your warm jackets and gloves and make your way to a local ice rink. Put on your skates and head out onto the ice! If your daughter is new to skating, go slowly so she's safe and relaxed. Hold hands and let your daughter set the pace. Praise her for her efforts. Be encouraging if she has trouble staying on her feet (or if she has to be patient with all of *your* tumbles on the ice!).

If your daughter is an experienced skater, give her the fun of showing you some pointers to improve your own skating skills. Give her a chance to perform for you and show you her talents.

Wrap up your skating date with some hot cocoa and time to talk and pray together.

Grow

Skating can be both nerve-wracking and exciting—you don't always know if you're going to lose your footing and end up flat on your back! It helps to have someone to hold on to for balance.

Sometimes in life we feel like we're going to slip and fall too. We can get tripped up by tough decisions, disappointments, conflict with others, and the temptation to make wrong choices. We can forget to lean on God for wisdom. We can get carried away with our own ideas and ignore what God's Word says about how to live.

It's reassuring to know that God both plans our steps and keeps us steady when the path of our life is "slippery." Psalm 37:24 tells us, "Though he may stumble, he will not fall, for the LORD upholds him with his hand." Psalm 55:22 says to "cast your cares on the LORD and he will sustain you; he will never let the righteous be shaken." When we don't know what to do, God's Word is a "lamp to my feet and a light to my path" (Ps. 119:105 ESV).

Talk with your daughter and make a list of any challenges, temptations, or decisions that could be tripping either of you up right now. Take some time to pray about these things right now!

Dear Father,

Thank you for your promises to keep us steady when life might make us stumble. Thank you for loving us so much that we can run to you with all our worries. Please keep us close to you—help us talk to you about everything we're going through. Teach us to read your Word when we don't know what to do. Help us to trust you with everything and follow you as you lead. We love you! Amen.

29

We All Scream for Ice Cream

☛ Grab

- » Two pint-sized food storage bags
- » Two gallon-sized food storage bags
- » 1 cup half-and-half
- » ¼ cup sugar
- » 1 tsp. vanilla
- » Kosher salt or rock salt
- » Ice

Go

In each of the two pint-sized food storage bags, have your daughter carefully pour ½ cup of half-and-half, 2 tablespoons of sugar, and ½ teaspoon of vanilla. Seal the bags tightly. Fill each of the gallon-sized bags half full of ice and sprinkle about ½ cup of salt over the ice. Place the smaller bags into the gallon-sized bags and seal securely. Shake the bags for about five minutes until the mixture has thickened into ice cream.

Remove the smaller bags from the larger bags of ice, rinse off the salty water, and cut off a lower corner of each small bag. Squeeze the ice cream from the bags into bowls and enjoy!

🌱 Grow

It's fascinating watching a sloppy bag of cream and sugar transform into a thick, delicious dessert. Sometimes we're a lot like that—when life "shakes us up," it changes us! Unexpected events, whether exciting or upsetting, force us to change our perspective and face how *not* in control we are of our lives. The great thing is that God promises to use every surprise and tough situation to grow our faith and make us more like Jesus.

God promises that not only can we survive hard situations, we can thrive! James 1:2–4 reminds us:

> Consider it pure joy, my brothers and sisters, whenever you face trials of many kinds, because you know that the testing of your faith produces perseverance. Let perseverance finish its work so that you may be mature and complete, not lacking anything.

God uses our trials to build our trust and make us "grow up" in him—that's something to be excited about! James continues by saying, "Blessed is the one who perseveres under trial because, having stood the test, that person will receive the crown of life that the Lord has promised to those who love him" (v. 12). Wow. Such awesome promises. No wonder we can have joy in the tough times!

Dear Lord,

Thank you for allowing challenges to come our way. If everything was easy all the time, we would never learn to trust and depend on you. We would never learn to hang in there and grow. We wouldn't have the chance to stand the test and receive your crown of life. Fill us with joy and excitement about the work you're doing in us as we are tested. Thank you for your love! Amen.

30

Diving In

☞ Grab

» Towels
» Swimsuits
» Goggles

» Pool toys such as foam noodles, dive rings, and floats

Go

Have a swimmingly great time at the pool! Throw dive rings for your daughter to find and tow her around the deep end with a foam noodle. Be a "shark" and chase your "minnow" in a game of tag. If your daughter is a beginning swimmer, praise her for every effort to put her face in the water or jump to you from the side of the pool. If she's more experienced in the water, have swimming races or play Marco Polo. See who can hold their breath underwater for the longest time, or who can float on their back or tread water the longest.

When swimming time is over, dry off and grab a snack together.

☸ Grow

Take this challenge together: count how many Bible stories you can think of that involve water! Many of these stories, such as Noah and the great flood, Jonah and the whale, and Peter walking on the water to Jesus, show the incredible power of God.

Ephesians 1:19 tells us that not only is God's power incredible, he shares it with *us*! It is his "incomparably great power for us who believe." How do you need God's power today? For healing? For strength in a hard situation? For the courage to share his gospel with others? Be encouraged. "For God gave us a spirit not of fear but of power and love and self-control" (2 Tim. 1:7 ESV).

God's love is great—he didn't leave us alone in the world to fend for ourselves. He cares about every struggle we'll ever face. He shares his mighty power with us to get us through anything. "You, God, are awesome in your sanctuary; the God of Israel gives power and strength to his people. Praise be to God!" (Ps. 68:35).

Dear God,

Your power is too great to understand! With your power you created the universe and raised your Son Jesus from the dead. Such incredible power is surely enough to handle our problems today. Please help us with our challenges. We have hard work to do. People can be difficult to get along with or forgive. We don't always have what we need. Show us your power in every situation. Teach us to trust you and depend on your strength. You are awesome! Amen.

31

Nature Hike

☞ Grab

» Walking shoes
» Binoculars
» Camera
» Field guide or bird-watching book

» Plastic bag
» Notebook and pen
» Water bottles

Go

Travel together to a nature preserve or state park that has a walking trail. Take your time walking down the trail. Encourage your daughter to walk quietly and be observant. Listen carefully for sounds that indicate wildlife around you. Use your binoculars to get an up-close look at birds or squirrels in the trees. Use your camera to take pictures of beautiful flowers or scenery. Collect pretty stones or leaves as keepsakes (as long as you don't damage any plants or break any park regulations). Use your notebook as a field journal to jot down which living creatures and unique trees and plants you spot on your hike, bugs included!

ᐖ Grow

If you'd hiked the trail with the end in mind, you would have missed out on the beauty and surprises that nature holds. Slowing down to look and listen brings great rewards.

The same is true with how we see—or don't see—God. When we get focused on our busy schedule and just getting through the day, we can miss out on lots of "God sightings."

Ask each other these questions:

> The greatest gift I ever had came from God, and I call him Dad!
>
> Author Unknown

» How has God answered a prayer this week?

» How did God protect me this week?

» What unexpected blessing did God give me this week?

» When could I have talked to God about a difficult situation this week, but I didn't because I was busy or distracted?

God has made an amazing promise: "Never will I leave you; never will I forsake you" (Heb. 13:5). Sometimes we need to quiet ourselves and remember who he is and how he works so faithfully in our lives. "Be still, and know that I am God" (Ps. 46:10). Take a deep breath, "be still," and spend a few moments praying together.

Dear God,

Thank you for staying so close to us. Thank you for never leaving us on our own. You care about every detail of our lives and watch over us each moment. Thank you for your beautiful creation that we were able to enjoy on our date. Just as we kept our eyes and ears open to notice wildlife today, give us eyes to see you! Don't let us miss the ways you answer prayer, bless us, and protect us each and every day. We want to be able to praise you for all your ways. We love you! Amen.

32

Paints, Pots, and Plants

☞ Grab

- » Terra-cotta flowerpot with saucer
- » Acrylic craft paints
- » Paint brushes and sponges
- » Stencils, masking tape

- » Paint smock or oversized T-shirt
- » Potting soil
- » Small flower or plant
- » Car keys

Go

Make your way to a local garden center with your daughter. Choose a medium-sized terra-cotta flowerpot and saucer. Have your daughter select a small flower or houseplant that she would like to plant in the pot.

Once you've returned home, have your daughter protect her clothes by wearing a paint smock. Cover your work area with newspaper. Have your daughter use a larger paintbrush to cover the flowerpot with a coat of paint. Then, when the base coat is dry, let her imagination take over! Perhaps she'll make stripes by sticking strips of masking tape onto the pot and painting between the lines of tape. Maybe she'll want to use stencils or make her own designs with brushes or sponges. She can even finger paint or make a colorful handprint.

When the pot is completely decorated and dry, have your daughter carefully spoon potting soil into the bottom of the pot. Place the flower or plant in the center and fill in the pot with more soil. Have your daughter carefully water the flower.

Work together to rinse out the brushes and clean up the "gardening" mess. Find a sunny spot to place the flowerpot—or even better, give someone a wonderful surprise by making it a gift!

🌱 Grow

The flower you found at the garden center was in a small plastic container. Were the roots beginning to grow out of the bottom of the container or becoming twisted around themselves? The flower didn't have what it needed to survive for long until you came and gave it a better pot where it could thrive.

Ask your daughter the following questions:

> » What does the flower need to grow? (water, sunlight, soil, etc.)
> » What do *you* need to grow? (food, sleep, safety, etc.)

It is God's plan for your daughter to grow not just in size, but in wisdom and in her relationship with God. In 2 Peter 3:18, we are encouraged to "grow in the grace and knowledge of our Lord and Savior Jesus Christ." Rather than soil, water, and sunlight, we need prayer, time in the Word, and encouragement from other Christians. How are you growing your faith this week?

Dear Father,

Thank you for helping my daughter grow each day. I see her becoming taller and stronger, learning a lot at school, and becoming closer to the friends and family in her life. Thank you for planting a "seed" of faith in her heart. Please "water" this seed by teaching her to pray and read the Bible all the time. Surround her with others who love you and will encourage her to follow you. Help both of us to grow in "the grace and knowledge of our Lord" until the day we see you in heaven. We love you so much! Amen.

33

Sharing Our Blessings

☞ Grab

» Nonperishable groceries
» Car keys

Go

Call your local food pantry or homeless shelter to find out when you can come and volunteer. Bring a bag of groceries along with you to donate. Work together with your daughter to help fill food boxes, make sandwiches, serve a meal, or participate in a worship service. Set an example for your daughter by being friendly and willing to help in any way that's needed. Find out about future opportunities to work with the organization.

When you have finished helping out, stop for a soda and talk together.

ＷＧＲＯＷ Grow

Ask each other the following questions:

» How did it feel to see people who didn't have enough food?
» Did you feel shy about talking to the people who came for help?
» Did seeing the needs of others make you more thankful for what you have?

» Was helping out today fun? Would you like to volunteer in the future?

Jesus was always concerned with the physical needs of the people he met. He healed the sick and fed thousands. Read Matthew 25:31–40:

> When the Son of Man comes in his glory, and all the angels with him, he will sit on his glorious throne. All the nations will be gathered before him, and he will separate the people one from another as a shepherd separates the sheep from the goats. He will put the sheep on his right and the goats on his left.
>
> Then the King will say to those on his right, "Come, you who are blessed by my Father; take your inheritance, the kingdom prepared for you since the creation of the world. For I was hungry and you gave me something to eat, I was thirsty and you gave me something to drink, I was a stranger and you invited me in, I needed clothes and you clothed me, I was sick and you looked after me, I was in prison and you came to visit me."
>
> Then the righteous will answer him, "Lord, when did we see you hungry and feed you, or thirsty and give you something to drink? When did we see you a stranger and invite you in, or needing clothes and clothe you? When did we see you sick or in prison and go to visit you?"
>
> The King will reply, "Truly I tell you, whatever you did for one of the least of these brothers and sisters of mine, you did for me."

When we serve others, we are serving Jesus himself! What a wonderful way to show him how much we love him.

Dear Lord,

Thank you for the blessings you have given us! We haven't had to go hungry and we've always had a place to sleep at night. Thank you for giving us the chance to share with others today. Please help each and every person that we saw today come to know you as their

Savior. Help them to trust you and live for you. Give them the food and shelter that they need. If they are sick and need healing, please make them well. Provide for the ministry so they can continue to care for everyone that comes for help. Give us compassionate hearts for those who don't have what they need each day—we want to help more and more! Thank you again for all the many ways you have blessed our family. Your love is awesome! Amen.

34

Deck the Halls

☞ Grab

» Miniature artificial Christmas tree
» Small string of battery-powered lights
» Beads
» Colorful pipe cleaners

» Curling ribbon
» Various miniature ornaments
» Your daughter's baby book or scrapbook

Go

Play some Christmas carols, make some hot cocoa, and get in the holiday spirit! Work together to bend the branches of the Christmas tree into the right shape. Wind the string of lights through the branches. Let your daughter string beads onto pipe cleaners and wrap them around the tree branches to resemble garlands. Tie curling ribbon to the ends of the branches. Use scissors to curl the ends of the ribbon. Hang the miniature ornaments on the tree and turn on the lights!

☗ Grow

In the days before Christmas, we remember the amazing story of the birth of Jesus. We read the story of how Mary discovered she would become the mother of the Savior of the world. She knew it would be an extraordinary experience to see the Son of God grow up before her eyes. (See Luke chapter 1 to read the full story and Mary's song of praise.)

Think back on the time when you were expecting the arrival of your own child. Take some time to describe the excitement and other feelings in your heart when you knew she was coming. Talk about how you chose her name, the place where she was born, and what your first moments with her were like.

Were you there at the hospital when she was born? Or did you have an amazing introduction when she was adopted? What were your hopes and dreams about becoming the father of a little girl? Take some time to look through your daughter's scrapbook and reminisce about her babyhood.

> **Dad to Dad**
>
> *This is definitely a touchy-feely date, but one every dad should have with his daughter. It means the world to a child to know they were wanted even before they were born.*

Dear Father,

Thank you for the incredible gift of Jesus, who was born as a baby to come into the world and save us. Thank you for the gift of my own daughter. You know how much I love her because you're her Father too! It is a privilege to be her dad. Help me to cherish her, watch over her, and point her to you. Amen.

35

Pets and Pics

☞ Grab

» Camera
» Walking shoes
» Computer and printer

» Stapler
» Markers

Go

It's time for a walk! Head out into your neighborhood with your camera and keep your eyes open for any creatures you can see, whether family pets or wildlife. Capture a photo of each animal, bird, or bug you encounter. Allow your daughter to be the photographer as much as possible.

Take your camera home and load the photos onto your computer. Print a copy of all the pictures you took today. Staple the pictures together to make a picture book. Work with your daughter to label each of the pictures. She can write what kind of animal or bug it is and even choose an imaginary name for each one. On the back of the book, write your names and the date.

⚜ Grow

Ask your daughter the following questions:

» Which kind of animal did we see the most?
» Which one was the funniest? Cutest? Ugliest?
» Which animal would be the most fun to play with?

Most girls are complete and total animal lovers! It's a wonderful thing, because they have a continually fresh appreciation for the variety of God's creation. Share this passage with her:

> And God said, "Let the water teem with living creatures, and let birds fly above the earth across the vault of the sky." So God created the great creatures of the sea and every living thing with which the water teems and that move about in it, according to their kinds, and every winged bird according to its kind. And God saw that it was good. God blessed them and said, "Be fruitful and increase in number and fill the water in the seas, and let the birds increase on the earth." And there was evening, and there was morning—the fifth day.
>
> And God said, "Let the land produce living creatures according to their kinds: livestock, the creatures that move along the ground, and the wild animals, each according to its kind." And it was so. God made the wild animals according to their kinds, the livestock according to their kinds, and all the creatures that move along the ground according to their kinds. And God saw that it was good. (Gen. 1:20–25)

Enter our children's world. Be intentional about knowing more about who they are and what influences their lives.

Jay Payleitner, *52 Things Kids Need from a Dad*

God enjoys the living creatures of the earth too! He made them all and declared them "good." He wants us to obey him by caring for the animals of the world. Take some time to thank God for the amazing creatures he has made.

Dear God,

Your creation is incredible! Each living thing is an example of how brilliant you are. Thank you for giving us this world to enjoy. Please give us wisdom for how to be the best caretakers of your earth that we can be. Help us to stand up for creatures that can't protect themselves. Help us, too, to be loving owners of the pets in our care. We want to live up to the responsibility you have entrusted to us. Amen.

36

Creative Cookies

☞ Grab

» Refrigerated sugar cookie dough
» Cookie cutters
» Flour
» Vanilla frosting
» Various sprinkles and colored sugar

» Small, colorful candies such as Skittles or M&Ms
» Aprons
» Paper and pencil

Go

Have your daughter put on an apron to protect her clothes (and let her pick out one for you!). Following the directions on the package of cookie dough, roll out the dough and cut out shapes with cookie cutters. Dip the cookie cutters in flour first to prevent the dough from sticking to them. Arrange the cookie dough cut-outs on baking sheets and bake according to the directions. Place cookies on a cooling rack or paper towels to cool.

When all of the cookies are baked and cooled, place them on a large tray and spread them with frosting. Use your creativity and add sprinkles, colored sugar, and candies. Finally, enjoy the best part of cookie baking: eating them!

᭠ Grow

Decorated cookies are awesome because you get layer upon layer of sugar—the cookie, the frosting, and the sprinkles combine for a great sugar rush! I'm sure your daughter brings her own "sugar rush" when she bats those eyelashes and shares her hugs with you.

While you're enjoying your cookies together, make a list on paper of all the sweet things she has said or done in the last few days. Was she friendly to a neighbor? Did she do some chores without being reminded? Did you get a big hug when you came home from work? Did she share a toy with a brother or sister?

When we belong to God he fills our hearts with his love. "By this all people will know that you are my disciples, if you have love for one another" (John 13:35 ESV).

Pray together and thank God for the gift of your daughter. Praise him for putting love in her heart for others. Thank him for the sweetness she brings to your life!

Dear Lord,

Thank you for the sweetness and love in my daughter's heart. It is amazing to watch the way she cares about others and shares her heart with me. Thank you for the chance to spend some time together today. Please continue to grow your love in each of us. Show us how to serve the people around us in your name. We want to be like Jesus! Amen.

37

Sidewalk Fun

☞ Grab

» Large paintbrushes
» Bucket of water
» Sidewalk chalk

» Jump rope
» Hula hoop

Go

Who knew an ordinary sidewalk could be so much *fun* on a sunny day? Fill the bucket with water and use a paintbrush to "paint" on the dry pavement of your sidewalk or driveway. How long do the pictures last before they dry up and fade away? Can you paint the whole alphabet before the "A" disappears?

Have your daughter lie down on the sidewalk and trace her outline with sidewalk chalk. Use different colors of chalk to fill in the details of her face, hair, and clothes.

Use the chalk to draw hopscotch and four-square games on the sidewalk. Get out the jump rope and compete to see how many hops you can each take before you lose your step. Time your daughter to see how long she can spin a hula hoop before it falls to the ground. Maybe she'll set a personal record today!

If it's a hot day, cool down by washing the chalk off the sidewalk (and each other) with the garden hose. Enjoy a cold drink of lemonade or a popsicle and have fun talking together.

☘ Grow

Was it a great day for fun in the sun? A bright, sunshiny day can remind us of Jesus, the Light of the World. John 8:12 says,

> When Jesus spoke again to the people, he said, "I am the light of the world. Whoever follows me will never walk in darkness, but will have the light of life."

Just like we expect the sun to come up every morning, we know God is faithful to be there for us every day. Just like the sun gives us light and warmth to survive, God gives us what we need to live forever. Nothing sinful can hide in the light, and God is truth and goodness all the time. Whenever you have fun in the sunshine, remember the Light and praise him!

Dear Father,

Thank you for this beautiful day to enjoy the sunshine you made. It's so much fun to play with my daughter! Thank you for being our light. You have saved us from a life of darkness without you. We love you so much! Amen.

38

Can She Build It? Yes She Can!

☞ Grab

» One 1-foot-square wooden
   board, at least ½-inch thick
» 4 feet of narrow wooden
   molding
» Hammer and nails
» Small saw
» Ruler
» Small flowerpot saucer
» Wild birdseed

Go

A platform bird feeder can be made by creating a wooden tray with a board and pieces of molding. Cut molding into four 1-foot pieces. Your daughter can help measure, mark, and saw through the molding with your help. Praise her for her efforts, even if she has trouble cutting smoothly or straight.

Nail cut pieces of molding around the top edges of the square board to form the sides. You may need to get the nails started, then your daughter can finish hammering them in the rest of the way. Encourage her to hammer with two hands, or to keep one hand out of the way so she doesn't end up with a hurt finger!

Find a great spot for your bird feeder. Perhaps it could rest on top of a large rock or an upside-down flowerpot, or place it on the railing of your deck. Have your daughter set the flowerpot saucer in the center of the bird feeder and fill it with water—you have a mini birdbath! She can sprinkle a scoop of birdseed around the tray along with slices of fruit or unsalted nuts.

Have a great time observing your bird feeder together and keeping it supplied with fresh food and water for your feathered friends.

> **Dad to Dad**
>
> *If you would rather not do this activity at home, check out your local home improvement store. Often, monthly classes are offered for kids that include projects like making bird feeders.*

Grow

If you keep your feeder stocked with fresh food and water, the birds in your yard will become daily visitors. It's a great experience to be a part of meeting their needs and observing their habits. God is attentive to us in the same way: he makes sure we have what we need and he is constantly watching our coming and going. The Bible says we can be encouraged by the way he takes care of the birds he has made.

> Are not five sparrows sold for two pennies? Yet not one of them is forgotten by God. Indeed, the very hairs of your head are all numbered. Don't be afraid; you are worth more than many sparrows. (Luke 12:6–7)

It's comforting to know that our Father never takes his eyes off of us. He knows every detail of our lives and just what we need. Doesn't that take a weight off your shoulders?

Dear Father,
Thank you for your amazing love and care for us. Just like you watch over the smallest living things, you never take your eyes off of us. Help us to trust you with everything. Fill our hearts with peace as our faith in you grows. We love you! Amen.

39

Paint Her Room

☞ Grab

» Paint to cover a wall or an entire room

» Paintbrushes and rollers

» Paint trays, drop cloth

» Masking tape

Go

Take your daughter to a local paint or home improvement store. Have fun choosing a paint color that makes your daughter say "Wow!" Select a durable, washable paint that can stand up to childhood. While you're there, pick up any other painting supplies you'll need to do the job.

Once you're home, move as many pieces of furniture and other belongings necessary to make room for your painting project. Change into clothing that can get splattered! Work with your daughter to spread the drop cloth and apply tape around windows and woodwork to protect from drips. Grab brushes and begin painting around the edges of the ceiling, baseboards, doorways, etc. Have a damp cloth handy to wipe up any "oops" that happen.

Once the edges are painted, have your daughter use a brush or roller to paint the walls. Don't worry about perfection; extra coats of paint can cover most flaws. Let her have fun doing as much as she'd like. Enjoy her pride and satisfaction in transforming her room!

🌱 Grow

Even though it's still your daughter's same space in the same house, it's amazing how a fresh coat of paint can make a room feel brand new. Ask your daughter the following questions:

> A father carries pictures where his money used to be.
>
> **Author Unknown**

» How does the color you chose make you feel? Is it relaxing? Exciting? Cozy?

» What does the color remind you of? A certain flower? A favorite shirt? A place you've visited?

» With a new color, does your room feel more unique? Do you think the color shows your personality? How?

Read the following verse together:

Therefore, if anyone is in Christ, he is a new creation. The old has passed away; behold, the new has come. (2 Cor. 5:17 ESV)

The same thing happens with us when we give our lives to Christ. We have the same physical body we always had, but God makes our thoughts, feelings, and attitudes brand-new. Old fears, bad habits, and a hopeless future are transformed as we're made more like Christ and have the hope of heaven. Ask each other how you have been "made new" since you found Jesus. How have your thoughts, attitudes, and actions changed as his children?

Dear God,

Thank you for making us your new creations! We know that we were lost before you found us and gave us hope. Please keep working in us—we want to look more and more like Jesus. Amen!

40

It's a Jungle Out There

☞ Grab

» Car keys
» Zoo admission
» Snacks and water bottles

» Sunscreen
» Walking shoes
» Camera

Go

Hop, crawl, or fly together to the zoo! Look over the zoo map and mark the exhibits that are a must-see. Let your daughter take the lead and have an amazing time checking out each animal habitat. Take turns with the camera. (She'll have fun telling everyone that her photo of the ape is really a picture of you!)

Grow

During a snack break, ask each other these questions:

» Of the animals we've seen, which would you like to pet the most?
» Which one would be fun to take home?
» Which one was the most scary? Ugly?
» Which animal habitat looked like fun to play in?
» If you could have any job at the zoo, which would be the most fun?
» If you were an animal, what do you think you would be?

Each animal has a unique habitat that meets its individual needs. Zoologists put huge amounts of study and effort into creating ideal environments where each animal can thrive.

God has placed us in just the right setting to live too!

From one man he made all the nations, that they should inhabit the whole earth; and he marked out their appointed times in history and the boundaries of their lands. God did this so that they would seek him and perhaps reach out for him and find him, though he is not far from any one of us. "For in him we live and move and have our being." (Acts 17:26–28)

God knew when we would be born and exactly where we should live. He had a purpose for our time and place: that we could find him as our Savior!

Dear Father,

Thank you that our lives aren't an accident. You knew exactly when and where we should be in this world so that we could find you. Thank you for the beautiful world you made and for all of the amazing creatures in it. Please remind us as we look at them in their habitats that you are in control. Your ways are perfect and you have loved us from the beginning of time. Amen!

41

A Real Page-Turner

☛ Grab

» Book-buying allowance
» Car keys

Go

Travel together to a local bookstore (hopefully one with a coffee shop!). Take your daughter's lead and browse the shelves together. Is she interested in a suspenseful mystery? A funny animated story? A historical drama? A colorful picture book? Create a "maybe list" as you browse and then allow your daughter to choose a book that excites her.

Take your purchase to the coffee shop or a favorite spot for a snack. Get something hot to drink and a sweet treat. Take some time to read the beginning part of your daughter's story to her, or take turns reading paragraphs or pages to each other.

❦ Grow

Sharing a story is a great way to connect. Ask your daughter these questions:

» What do you like about the different characters in the story?
» Which character would be a good friend in real life? Why?
» What are some things you have in common with the characters?

» How do you think the main character needs to grow or change?

» Are there any qualities of the characters that you wish you had?

It's fun to read about imaginary or historical characters and get a window into a different world than our own. Reading gives us the chance to time travel without leaving our chairs. It's amazing how a limitless number of people, places, and ideas can be expressed through a string of symbols on a piece of paper.

God has shown himself to us through words—the words of the Bible and *the* Word, Jesus. "In the beginning was the Word, and the Word was with God, and the Word was God" (John 1:1). He gave us the gift of words and language so we could receive his truth. Our ability to speak lets us pray, and reading opens the door to the best book ever—the Bible!

All Scripture is God-breathed and is useful for teaching, rebuking, correcting and training in righteousness, so that the servant of God may be thoroughly equipped for every good work. (2 Tim. 3:16–17)

God's Word can change our hearts and change our lives. Talk about ways you can "hide his word in your hearts" (see Ps. 119:11) starting today!

Dear God,

Thank you for the gift of words. We are so glad we have a way to talk to you and read your truth in the Bible. Please help us use our words carefully. We want to encourage others and speak in love and kindness to everyone we meet. Teach us to love your Word so we can be more like Jesus. Amen!

42

Bike Ride

☞ Grab

» Bikes and helmets
» Water bottles

Go

This won't be the Tour de France, but it will be fun! Build anticipation for the ride by having a bike inspection in the garage. Make sure the tires are at the right pressure, that your daughter's seat is adjusted to a comfortable height, and that the chains are clean and lubricated. Choose a route, whether on the road or on a bike trail. Avoid lots of intersections to cross or busy streets if your daughter is a beginner. Take a few minutes to talk about bike safety and put on your helmets.

Decide who will lead and let your daughter set the pace. As you travel, stop from time to time to enjoy a nice view or have a drink of water. Keep distance in mind; you'll want to save up enough energy for the return trip to your home or vehicle.

If your daughter is inexperienced, she may need several reminders to stay to the right side of the road or trail. Have patience with her slower pace and stamina. Once you return home and park the bikes, give her a hug and let her know how thankful you are to have time with her.

🌱 Grow

A bike is very different from a car: you travel under your own power. This limits the speed and distance you can travel, and the only thing between you and the pavement is your helmet.

This is a little bit like life. We can go through our days depending on our own limited strength or on the mighty power of God. It is God's desire for us to depend on him more and more. With him all things are possible (see Matt. 19:26). He doesn't want us to settle for less. On our own, we don't have the power to overcome sin or know God's best plan. We need him for wisdom and courage. Even our goodness depends on him. What do you need to depend on God for today?

> It is admirable for a man to take his son fishing, but there is a special place in heaven for the father who takes his daughter shopping.
>
> **John Sinor**

Dear God,

Thank you for giving us your strength to lean on. Please be the power in our lives! We want your goodness, wisdom, and love. Our own efforts to be like Jesus will fail every time. Give us the humility to ask for your help and hold on tight to you. We don't want a fake righteousness that we make on our own. We want the real thing—hearts filled with your Spirit. Amen!

43

Video Games

☞ Grab

» Video game console
» Age-appropriate games
» Popcorn

Go

Pop some popcorn, make sure you have some elbow room, and get your game on! Let your daughter choose the first game. Set the appropriate difficulty level for each of you and stay on the same team whenever possible. Set a timer for around twenty minutes per game, taking turns choosing what you will play next.

Between turns, enjoy some popcorn and high-fives for the winner. If you've been playing a sit-down game, take a minute to stretch and do some jumping jacks. Keep the focus on the fun rather than the competition. Encourage each other to be flexible and go with the flow if a game is difficult or is not a favorite.

☖ Grow

Do you ever get stuck on a game level and have to try it over and over before you finally succeed? That's a lot like life! The Bible compares our Christian life to running a race or fighting a fight. Sometimes you get really tired and just want to sit down on the side of the track and say "enough!" It can be hard to keep resisting temptation or to keep loving others even when they don't love us back. It's hard sometimes to do the right thing when everybody else is just living for themselves. It can be hard to trust in God when we've been waiting for an answer to prayer for what feels like forever.

God has great words of encouragement when we just want to quit.

> Therefore, since we are surrounded by such a great cloud of witnesses, let us throw off everything that hinders and the sin that so easily entangles. And let us run with perseverance the race marked out for us, fixing our eyes on Jesus, the pioneer and perfecter of faith. For the joy set before him he endured the cross, scorning its shame, and sat down at the right hand of the throne of God. Consider him who endured such opposition from sinners, so that you will not grow weary and lose heart. (Heb. 12:1–3)

> Do you not know?
> Have you not heard?
> The LORD is the everlasting God,
> the Creator of the ends of the earth.
> He will not grow tired or weary,
> and his understanding no one can fathom.
> He gives strength to the weary
> and increases the power of the weak.
> Even youths grow tired and weary,
> and young men stumble and fall;
> but those who hope in the LORD
> will renew their strength.
> They will soar on wings like eagles;
> they will run and not grow weary,
> they will walk and not be faint. (Isa. 40:28–31)

Dear Lord,

You know that sometimes we get tired and are tempted to throw in the towel. Whether it's struggling with a sin or getting along with a difficult person, we can't overcome on our own. Please give us your mighty strength when we are weak. Give us new motivation when we're ready to quit. Please keep us faithful to the end when we'll see your face. We love you! Amen.

44

Treasure Box

☞ Grab

» Washable tempera paints,
brushes
» Beads, glitter, feathers, ribbon
» Stickers, stick-on plastic gems

» Glue, scissors
» Wooden or papier-mâché box
with lid
» Newspaper

Go

Your daughter's treasure box will be a treasure in itself! Help her spread newspaper over your work area. Lay out all of the various craft supplies, paint, and glue. Provide her with a water cup for her paint brushes.

Follow her instructions as you work together to paint her box. Let her choose the colors. Let the paint dry, then begin gluing gems, ribbon, glitter, etc. onto the box. In this case, there cannot be too much of a good thing! When your daughter decides her box is complete, set it aside so the glue can dry.

᭦ Grow

While the box is drying, read the following verses:

Do not lay up for yourselves treasures on earth, where moth and rust destroy, and where thieves break in and steal, but lay up for yourselves treasures in heaven, where neither moth nor rust destroys and where thieves do not break in and steal. For where your treasure is, there your heart will be also. (Matt. 6:19–21 ESV)

Command them to do good, to be rich in good deeds, and to be generous and willing to share. In this way they will lay up treasure for themselves as a firm foundation for the coming age, so that they may take hold of the life that is truly life. (1 Tim. 6:18–19)

1. Work with your daughter to make a list of the treasures we try to store up on earth.
2. Brainstorm together to make a list of ways to give and share that "lay up for yourselves treasures in heaven."
3. Commit to using the treasure box to hold dollars and spare change that can add up to a wonderful gift to help others. Consider the church or organizations to which you may be able to donate your savings.
4. Pray together, thanking God for all the ways he has blessed you with "treasure" in your lives.

Dear Lord,

You have blessed us in every way! Please teach us to have thankful hearts and to see all of the ways you share your treasure with us each day. Please give us hearts that care for others. Please show us how you want us to share with those around us. Amen.

45

Science Lab

☞ Grab

- » Epsom salts
- » Food coloring
- » Wooden matchsticks
- » Clear soda
- » Black paper
- » Baby oil or mineral oil

- » Dish soap
- » Raisins
- » Pie plates
- » Plastic bottle with cap
- » Pepper

Go

For your first experiment, cut a piece of black construction paper to fit in the bottom of a pie plate. Stir one tablespoon of Epsom salts into ¼ cup of water until dissolved. Place the black paper in the pie plate and pour the liquid over it. Place the plate in the sun to dry. Once the water has evaporated, spiky salt crystals will have formed on the black paper.

While you're waiting for your salt crystals to form, start working on your second experiment. Fill a plastic bottle three-fourths full of baby oil or mineral oil. Stir food coloring into a cup of water. Fill the remainder of the bottle of oil with the colored water. Cap the bottle tightly, and have your daughter tip the bottle over to see colorful "blobs" move through the oil.

For experiment number three, fill a glass pie plate with water. Place several wooden matchsticks on the water. Have your daughter squeeze a drop of dish soap in the middle of the pie plate. Have fun watching the matchsticks shoot across the water. Fill the pie plate with fresh water and try this one again, this time sprinkling pepper into the water rather than matchsticks. The pepper will "run away" from the dish soap.

For your fourth experiment, fill a cup with clear soda such as 7–Up or Sprite. Drop in a few raisins and watch them bob up and down in the soda as carbonation bubbles attach to them.

> A father is always making his baby into a little woman. And when she is a woman he turns her back again.
>
> Enid Bagnold

〽 Grow

Just as our God never changes, he has set laws over his creation that do not change either. The sun rises and sets each day, a tomato seed produces a tomato, and a ball thrown into the air will eventually come down again.

God chose to reveal truths about himself in the world that he made. Anyone who has seen the earth has seen clues about the nature of God himself!

> For since the creation of the world God's invisible qualities—his eternal power and divine nature—have been clearly seen, being understood from what has been made, so that people are without excuse. (Rom. 1:20)

God wants all men to know him. In his kindness he has shown how real he is through the world he made. No one will be able to say that God could not be found!

Dear Father,

Thank you for your great love. You have shown yourself to us in so many ways—through the Bible, the testimony of other believers, the story of Jesus in history, and creation itself. Please give us eyes to see you in the world all around us. Teach us to appreciate the study of science as a way to see your hand in creation. You are awesome! Amen.

46

Playing with a Full Deck

☞ Grab

» Car keys
» Playing cards
» Variety of card games (Uno, Memory, Skip-Bo, Go Fish, etc.)

» Paper and pen
» Stickers

Go

Travel to a fast-food restaurant or ice cream parlor. Order a great snack and get ready to deal! Let your daughter choose the first card game and decide who will be the scorekeeper. Take the "loser goes first" approach when you start new rounds or games. Reward the winner of each game with a sticker to wear, and see who has the most stickers by the end of the date.

☽ Grow

Did you play Go Fish during your date today? It's a great game—if you don't have what you need, you just "go fishing" to fill up your hand with more cards.

Life is a little bit like that. Sometimes we don't have what we need. We need more energy, more time, more money, more help. In those times we have a loving Father to go to, for "my God will meet all your needs according to the riches of his glory in Christ Jesus" (Phil. 4:19).

» What are some ways that you have seen God provide in the past?

» Have you seen the Lord meet the needs of anyone you know recently?

» What are some needs each of you are struggling with right now?

» Is anyone you know going through a hardship today?

Take the burdens you have talked about straight to Jesus, right this moment!

Dear Father,

Thank you for caring about everything we go through. You are loving and always willing to listen. We thank you for your promise to take care of us and meet our needs. Today we really need you! Please help us and the ones we love. Teach us to trust you as we wait for you to provide. Amen.

---

15 Great Games to Play Together

Battleship	Mancala	Uno Attack
Candyland	Mastermind	Yahtzee
Farkle	Rat-a-Tat-Cat	
Guess Who?	Rory's Story Cubes	
Horse-opoly	The Scrambled	
Jenga	States of America	
Life	Set	

47

A Blast from the Past

☞ Grab

» Money
» Car keys

Go

Put on your walking shoes and prepare to step back in time! Find out the location and scheduled hours of your community's historical museum. Make the most of it by planning your visit during a special exhibit or presentation.

⚘ Grow

It's fascinating to get a glimpse into the past. So much was different—what people ate, how they dressed and how they styled their hair, the way they traveled, and what they did for fun.

Imagine yourselves in a different era:

» In what ways would life be more challenging than it is now?
» In what ways would life be easier?
» Does living in the past appeal to you? Why or why not?

Some things in life have always been the same. We always need food, clothing, transportation, and a roof over our heads. People have always had children and families. Sad things like sickness and natural disasters have come along, but fun holidays and celebrations have brought excitement throughout the ages.

Another thing that has never changed is mankind's need for a Savior. Romans 3:23 says, "All have sinned and fall short of the glory of God," and Romans 3:10 tells us, "There is no one righteous, not even one." However, God has always offered the hope of salvation to each person, "the hope of eternal life, which God, who does not lie, promised before the beginning of time" (Titus 1:2).

Read that again and really let it sink in! God has been offering the gift of salvation to every generation from the very beginning.

Thank you, Father, for placing us right where we are in the timeline of history. Thank you for making a way for our salvation through Jesus Christ. We know that just as you have been faithful to your children through all of history, you will continue to be faithful to us in the future. Help us to walk with you through every day we're given. Amen!

10 Things Your Daughter Needs to Hear from You

1. I love you!
2. You are beautiful.
3. God loves you, and I'm sure glad he gave you to me!
4. I would love to play with you.
5. Her special nickname.
6. You are so good at _____. (You fill in the blank.)
7. I'm so proud of you.
8. I'm here to help if you need me.
9. I'm sorry. Please forgive me.
10. Can I have a hug?

48

Indoor Campout

☞ Grab

» Blankets, sheets
» Sleeping bags, pillows
» Large rubber bands, clothespins
» Marshmallows, chocolate, graham crackers

» Flashlights
» Cooler
» Stories, games

Go

It's time to enjoy the great indoors! Work together to build your "tent." Arrange chairs or other furniture in a square. Use rubber bands and clothespins to fasten the corners of sheets and blankets to the furniture, creating a cozy, covered sleeping space. Arrange your sleeping bags and pillows inside. Let your daughter bring in as many wild creatures as she likes in the form of stuffed animals. Stock your tent with flashlights, storybooks, games, and whatever else you would like to have on hand for fun.

Make some s'mores in your microwave "campfire." Put a piece of chocolate on top of a graham cracker on a plate. Place a marshmallow on top of the chocolate and microwave it for a few seconds (watch carefully!) until it's puffed up and hot. Take the plate out of the microwave and quickly cover the marshmallow with another graham cracker. Enjoy the sweet stickiness!

Turn out the lights and settle into your tent for the night. Tell some jokes, play games, and read bedtime stories by flashlight.

𝕎 Grow

If you were camping on the highest mountain, God would know where you were. If you were on a ship in the middle of the ocean, he would be there. If you spelunked your way into the deepest cave, he would know exactly where you were. Your Father knows where you are right at this moment and is loving you more than you could ever imagine. Before you fall asleep, read the following Psalm together as a prayer to the Lord.

You have searched me, LORD,
and you know me.
You know when I sit and when I rise;
you perceive my thoughts from afar.
You discern my going out and my lying down;
you are familiar with all my ways.
Before a word is on my tongue
you, LORD, know it completely.
You hem me in—behind and before,
and you lay your hand upon me.
Such knowledge is too wonderful for me,
too lofty for me to attain.

Where can I go from your Spirit?
Where can I flee from your presence?
If I go up to the heavens, you are there;
if I make my bed in the depths, you are there.
If I rise on the wings of the dawn,
if I settle on the far side of the sea,
even there your hand will guide me,
your right hand will hold me fast.
If I say, "Surely the darkness will hide me
and the light become night around me,"
even the darkness will not be dark to you;
the night will shine like the day,
for darkness is as light to you.

For you created my inmost being;
you knit me together in my mother's womb.
I praise you because I am fearfully and wonderfully made;
your works are wonderful,
I know that full well. (Ps. 139:1–14)

49

Family Coat of Arms

☞ Grab

» Poster board
» Markers, scissors, glue, tape
» Beads, yarn, ribbon, etc.
» Colorful duct tape

» Family photographs
» Old magazines
» Wooden dowel

Go

There is no other family like yours, and it's time to celebrate it! Cut off the bottom corners of the poster board so it resembles the shape of a shield. Have your daughter write your family name in large letters across the top. Using strips of duct tape, divide your coat of arms into five sections. Have your daughter label each section with markers: family, faith, fun, food, and friends.

In the family section, attach photos or drawings of your family members (don't forget your extended family and the family pets!). Have your daughter write each of your names in different colors.

In the faith section, write the name of your place of worship. Attach a picture or worship bulletin from a recent service. Have your daughter make a cross out of toothpicks, beads, or whatever strikes her imagination, and fasten it to the banner. Attach a Bible verse that is meaningful to your family.

For the fun section, think about your family's favorite ways to have a good time. Cut out pictures from old magazines or have your daughter draw pictures of favorite sports, vacation spots, or other ways you relax as a family. Attach photos from past vacations, holidays, or birthday parties. Make this section crazy and fun!

I'm sure your family has some favorite treats and restaurants. Have your daughter create "food" out of construction paper and stick it onto the food section. Perhaps you have a favorite candy bar—attach the empty wrapper to your banner! Cut out the logo from a take-out menu or pizza box.

Finally, add photos and names of special family friends to the friends area. Which friends are like family to you? Who are your "two o'clock in the morning" friends that are always there when something major happens? Honor those special people by displaying them on your poster.

Take time to finish off your coat of arms by wrapping the outer edge of the poster with duct tape or trimming it with beads or stickers. Duct tape a wooden dowel to the upper edge on the back. Tie a string or ribbon to the ends of the dowel to serve as a hanger. Display your banner proudly in your home and enjoy sharing it with the rest of the family.

Grow

It was never God's intention for us to go through life alone. The love we hold for our family and friends is a taste of our amazing future: eternity with the entire family of God.

> See what great love the Father has lavished on us, that we should be called children of God! And that is what we are! (1 John 3:1)

Dear Lord,

Thank you for giving us a family and friends that care about us. Thank you for loving us through each of them. Teach us to love one another with patience, loyalty, kindness, and fun. Amen!

50

Go Fly a Kite

☞ Grab

» Kite with string, or materials to make a kite
» Blanket
» Drinks and a snack

Go

On a dry, breezy day, take your daughter to shop for a kite or have a good time making one yourself. Several basic patterns for kites that use household items can be found online by typing "make a simple kite" into your browser's search engine.

Travel to a grassy, open area. Stay away from trees and power lines. Have your daughter hold the kite above her head, downwind from you. While you hold the string, have your daughter let go of the kite as the wind catches it and it takes flight. This may take a few tries—be patient and see the humor in your efforts! Once your kite catches the air, gradually release more and more string to give it altitude. When it's flying well, hand the string over to your daughter and give her the thrill of flying it herself.

Get comfortable on your blanket to get a better view of the kite in the sky. Share a snack together and enjoy the outdoors.

When you're ready to finish kite flying for the day, have your daughter slowly wind the string around its spool to bring the kite in.

⚜ Grow

Did you feel a little jealous of your kite's ability to fly? Wouldn't the view from high up in the air be fantastic? It would be quite a rush to be caught up into the sky like a kite.

Can you imagine how the disciples felt when they saw Jesus ascend into the air to return to his Father in heaven? Acts 1:9–11 describes the scene:

> Fathers are a powerful, yet largely untapped resource in our society.
>
> Joe Kelly

> After he said this, he was taken up before their very eyes, and a cloud hid him from their sight.
>
> They were looking intently up into the sky as he was going, when suddenly two men dressed in white stood beside them. "Men of Galilee," they said, "why do you stand here looking into the sky? This same Jesus, who has been taken from you into heaven, will come back in the same way you have seen him go into heaven."

Jesus says that when he comes back for us someday we will meet him in the air.

> For the Lord himself will come down from heaven, with a loud command, with the voice of the archangel and with the trumpet call of God, and the dead in Christ will rise first. After that, we who are still alive and are left will be caught up together with them in the clouds to meet the Lord in the air. And so we will be with the Lord forever. Therefore encourage each other with these words. (1 Thess. 4:16–18)

For now we can see kites, clouds, and birds flying up in the sky. What a wonderful day it will be when we see our Savior coming for us in the air!

Dear Lord,

Thank you for giving us a day to look forward to when we'll see you face-to-face. Please give us patience while we wait! Give us the courage to share the good news of your salvation so that the people around us can be with you too. We love you and can't wait to see you! Amen.

51

Snow Day

☞ Grab

» Cold-weather gear
» Snow shovel
» Bucket
» Hot cocoa mix

» Spray bottle
» Water bottle
» Food coloring

Go

Let it snow, let it snow, let it snow! Fill your spray bottle and water bottle with cold water. Add a few drops of food coloring to each to make colorful water. Bundle up for cold weather and head outdoors to play in the white stuff.

Work together to build a snow dad and snow daughter. Personalize your snow-clones! Use your spray bottle of colored water to make rosy cheeks on their faces, or write your names on them by squirting colored water from the water bottle. Dress up your snow people with an old tie or work uniform for dad and an outgrown hoodie for daughter. Put mittens on their stick "arms" and create goofy expressions on their faces with buttons, carrots, or whatever is handy.

Build a snow fort or shelter together. Pack snow into a bucket to create snow blocks and stack them into a sturdy wall. Leave a gap in the blocks for a window. Place a couple of blocks inside to serve as chairs. Bring out some hot cocoa from the house and warm up in your shelter!

Use your colored water to paint a target on the ground. Have a contest to see who can throw the most snowballs into the target.

Finally, it wouldn't be a snow day without making some snow angels. Admire your creations and then get inside to thaw out!

Dad to Dad

If you don't live in a cold climate, you can still have a great time by making your own snow! Purchase snow powder at a craft store or sodium polyacrylate crystals at a garden supply store. Add water slowly to the powder and watch it expand into fluffy snow. You can even chill it in the freezer for a wintery effect. Put on your scarves, pour some hot cocoa, and have a wonderful do-it-yourself snow day!

Grow

There's nothing more exciting to a kid than waking up to an unexpected day off of school (and we should know since we're from Michigan!). Freshly fallen snow makes everything look clean and white—just perfect for making tracks with winter boots, skis, and sleds.

The Bible says that *we* can be as white as snow when God has done his work of cleansing us from sin. Isaiah 1:18 says, "Though your sins are like scarlet, they shall be as white as snow." Are there any sins weighing on your conscience today? Are they stealing your joy and keeping you from being close to God? Take a few moments to silently talk to God about these struggles. Follow David's example in Psalm 51 and pray his prayer to the Father:

> Have mercy on me, O God,
> according to your unfailing love;
> according to your great compassion
> blot out my transgressions.
> Wash away all my iniquity
> and cleanse me from my sin.

For I know my transgressions,
and my sin is always before me.
Against you, you only, have I sinned
and done what is evil in your sight;
so you are right in your verdict
and justified when you judge.
Surely I was sinful at birth,
sinful from the time my mother conceived me.
Yet you desired faithfulness even in the womb;
you taught me wisdom in that secret place.
Cleanse me with hyssop, and I will be clean;
wash me, and I will be whiter than snow. (vv. 1–7)

Thank you, Father! Amen.

52

Follow the Leader

☞ Grab

» Jump rope
» Outdoor toys
» Scooter or bike
» Basketball

» Wagon or yard cart
» Drinks and snacks
» Timer or stopwatch

Go

Set your timer or stopwatch for five minutes and begin your game of Follow the Leader. Dad starts out as leader, moving from one activity to the next. Perhaps you can jump rope ten times, bounce a basketball ten times, ride the scooter in a circle around the driveway, pull a wagon across the yard, swing from a tree branch three times, jump over rocks, and eat three potato chips. Be creative! See how many items in your yard you can jump over, run around, or crawl under. When the timer runs out, give your daughter a turn as the leader.

The same activities can also work as an obstacle course. Choose several activities to move through in a row. Time each other to see who can move through the course the fastest. Can your daughter jump rope, blow bubbles, spin a hula hoop, make a basket, run around the house, and bike to the end of the driveway faster than you?

✨ Grow

It's a lot of fun to follow someone in a game—you don't know where they'll take you next and sometimes their ideas are creative and hilarious.

It's not always wise to follow people in real life, however. We need to make wise choices about whose example we follow and whose plans we go along with. Read these verses together:

> Blessed is the person who does not
> follow the advice of wicked people,
> take the path of sinners,
> or join the company of mockers.
> Rather, he delights in the teachings of the LORD
> and reflects on his teachings day and night. (Ps. 1:1–2 GW)

> Do not be misled: "Bad company corrupts good character." (1 Cor. 15:33)

> Do not be yoked together with unbelievers. For what do righteousness and wickedness have in common? Or what fellowship can light have with darkness? (2 Cor. 6:14)

Together, make a list of the friends you have that bless you by pointing you to Christ. Thank God for these special people right now.

Dear God,

Thank you for giving us your Word to show us how to live. Thank you for giving us Christian friends to set a great example of following you. Please help us to make wise choices about who we admire and spend time with. Give us hearts that want to obey you and look like Jesus. Use us to encourage the people we care about to live for you in every way. Thanks that we don't have to walk our Christian lives on our own! You are so good to us. Amen!

53

Movie Night

☞ Grab

» Money
» Car keys

Go

Choose an age-appropriate "girly" film and head to the theater. (Don't worry, Dad, you will survive one chick flick!) Once you have your tickets and popcorn, enjoy the movie!

> **Dad to Dad**
> For an at-home date, see page 130 for a list of great video suggestions. Also, www.pluggedinonline.com provides helpful movie reviews as you select quality films for your family.

☖ Grow

After the film is over, take some time to talk about the movie together. Ask these questions:

» How did the main character seem great on the outside? (pretty, talented, etc.)
» How did the main character seem great on the inside? (kind, brave, generous, etc.)
» What do you think the main character wanted more than anything else?

» How do you think you would have handled the character's problems?

» Do you think the character was a good friend? How?

» Do you think the character had a loving family? In what ways?

» What would be fun about being that character?

» What would be hard about being that character?

What makes the story in a movie or a book so exciting is seeing how the characters overcome the danger and drama they're faced with. We may never find ourselves living in a fantasy world with imaginary creatures, having to solve a mystery or a crime, or discovering that we've been a prince or princess our whole lives and never knew it! However, we all know what it's like to have to stand by a friend and face challenges that seem too big to overcome.

If someone made a movie of *your* life, how would they describe you as the main character? How would they answer the questions listed above if they were talking about you and your family?

Hopefully, what others would see as they watched your life would be Jesus: his goodness, his joy, and his love shining through you.

You are the light of the world. A town built on a hill cannot be hidden. Neither do people light a lamp and put it under a bowl. Instead they put it on its stand, and it gives light to everyone in the house. In the same way, let your light shine before others, that they may see your good deeds and glorify your Father in heaven. (Matt. 5:14–16)

Dear Father,

As other people watch the "movie" of our lives, let our characters be known for looking like you. Give us your love, your goodness, and your wisdom as we face the challenges that come our way. Please let us be a light in the darkness that draws people to you.

We want to share you with others so they can be saved. Thank you for writing our story. We love you! Amen.

20 Movies to Watch with Your Daughter

Because of Winn-Dixie

Bolt

The Chronicles of Narnia

Despicable Me

Felicity: An American Girl Adventure

Flicka

Fly Away Home

Kit Kittredge: An American Girl

Letters to God

A Little Princess

Little Women

Mandie and the Cherokee Treasure

Mandie and the Secret Tunnel

Molly: An American Girl on the Home Front

Night at the Museum

Nim's Island

Ramona and Beezus

Samantha: An American Girl Holiday

Soul Surfer

Up

54

Garage Sales

☞ Grab

» Money
» Car keys

Go

Check your local paper to find ads for garage sales in your area. Give your daughter a spending allowance and a challenge: find something to play with, something to wear, something useful, and something to share.

Hop in the car and make your way from sale to sale. Give your daughter time to browse at her own pace. Encourage her to stick with the challenge and not buy every stuffed animal she sees!

Once she has found her four items, stop for ice cream or a cold drink and talk together.

⋎ Grow

Have you ever heard the expression, "One man's trash is another man's treasure"? Today you found things that weren't useful to their owner any more. To you, though, the items were new and exciting.

Do you ever feel like you've been "garage-saled"? Have you ever been rejected by a friend or left out of the group? Have you ever been picked last for a team, not had a part in a play or concert, or been left off the invitation list to a party? It hurts to feel like you're on the outside looking in.

God loves us so much that we're never left out of his family. With him, we always belong! It was really important to him that kids be included, even when he was in popular demand as a teacher on earth. Read this story from Mark 10:13–16:

> People were bringing little children to Jesus for him to place his hands on them, but the disciples rebuked them. When Jesus saw this, he was indignant. He said to them, "Let the little children come to me, and do not hinder them, for the kingdom of God belongs to such as these. Truly I tell you, anyone who will not receive the kingdom of God like a little child will never enter it." And he took the children in his arms, placed his hands on them and blessed them.

God always wants you. He's never too busy to listen. He is patient with our mistakes and understands our weaknesses. We don't have to be popular, smart, athletic, or stylish to get his attention. Best of all, he gives us that kind of love *forever*. Dad, pray this prayer from Ephesians 3:14–19 over your daughter as you commit her to God:

> For this reason I kneel before the Father, from whom every family in heaven and on earth derives its name. I pray that out of his glorious riches he may strengthen you with power through his Spirit in your inner being, so that Christ may dwell in your hearts through faith. And I pray that you, being rooted and established in love, may have power, together with all the Lord's holy people, to grasp how wide and long and high and deep is the love of Christ, and to know this love that surpasses knowledge—that you may be filled to the measure of all the fullness of God.

Amen!

55

Mad Libs

☞ Grab

» Book of mad libs for kids, pen or pencil

» Money
» Car keys

Go

Take your daughter to a local bookstore to select and purchase a book of mad libs for kids. Then take your mad libs book to a favorite fast-food restaurant. While you're enjoying your burgers and fries, have a hilarious time filling in the blanks in the book. Depending on your daughter's reading and writing level, take turns writing in the words and reading the completed stories. If you're feeling really creative, make up your own mad lib story about a day with your daughter!

❧ Grow

With mad libs, you never know how the story will turn out. The only thing you know is that it will be funny and ridiculous! Our lives are actually a story, too, and the author of our story is God. While mad libs can be pure nonsense, God promises that our lives will have meaning and value if he is in control. Read these verses together:

> Surely your goodness and love will follow me all the days of my life, and I will dwell in the house of the LORD forever. (Ps. 23:6)

All the days ordained for me were written in your book before one of them came to be. (Ps. 139:16)

"For I know the plans I have for you," declares the LORD, "plans to prosper you and not to harm you, plans to give you hope and a future." (Jer. 29:11)

Dear Father,

Thank you that our lives here on this earth are not an accident—you created us as part of your sovereign plan! We are so grateful for the plans you have for each of us. We are excited to serve you in all the ways you have prepared for us. Please give us hearts eager to do your will and follow you each and every day. Thank you for your loving hand that guides our steps. Amen.

56

Prayer Mail

☞ Grab

» Blank note cards or index cards   » Tape
» Markers, stickers   » Car keys

Go

Make a list together of several people you can lift up to God in prayer. Think of neighbors, friends, your pastor, your daughter's school teachers and classmates, church friends, or family members that live nearby. Make a note card for each one. On the front of each card write, "We prayed for you today!" On the inside or the back of each card, work together to copy Isaiah 40:31:

> But those who hope in the LORD
> will renew their strength.
> They will soar on wings like eagles;
> they will run and not grow weary,
> they will walk and not be faint.

Have your daughter decorate the cards with stickers or her own drawings. Then gather the cards together and get ready for your prayer drive!

Drive together to the house of one of your friends or family members. Pull over and park the car. Spend a few moments praying for that special person. Ask for God's protection and healing, that their studies or work would be successful, and that they

In all my years of practice and of speaking to literally millions of people through radio and television and at seminars, one fact has impressed me as much as anything else: Fathers leave an indelible imprint on the lives of their daughters. They shape their daughters in ways so profound that many women live with unwritten rules they've never thought to question. These rules were ingrained into them so deeply, many women don't realize that though they may graduate from college, get married, and even give birth to a half-dozen males, they'll still never stop being Daddy's girl.

Kevin Leman, *What a Difference a Daddy Makes*

would have peace and joy in their homes. Thank God for making each person a part of your life and name the ways they have been a blessing to you. When you're finished praying, place a piece of tape on a card and have your daughter attach it to the person's door. Try to be anonymous as you do so—imagine what a fun surprise it will be for that person to find out they have been lifted up in prayer by a secret someone!

Travel from place to place until you've prayed for each person on your list and left a card for them. When you return to your own house, take a moment to pray for each other and the loved ones you share your home with.

Grow

The Bible tells us that we should never stop praying for each other!

And pray in the Spirit on all occasions with all kinds of prayers and requests. With this in mind, be alert and always keep on praying for all the Lord's people. (Eph. 6:18)

God cares about each person that you care about. He created each one and put them in your life as part of his plan. One way we can love our friends and family is to give them to God in prayer. It's exciting to see the way he listens to us and moves through the prayers of his people!

Dear Lord,

Thank you so much for our friends and family—you have put so much of your love into our lives through them. Please encourage them today by the cards we delivered and the prayers we offered up. If anyone is tired, give them strength. If someone is sick, please give them healing. If they are worried, give them your peace. If they are celebrating, give them hearts that praise you! Thank you for watching over each and every one of us. We love you! Amen.

57

Tower Time

☞ Grab

» Plastic building blocks, such as
Duplo bricks
» Wooden block-stacking game
» Plastic or paper cups
» Cardboard boxes of various sizes

» Duct tape, scissors, markers
» Crackers, cheese, lunch meat,
pickle slices
» Sandwich cookies

Go

Clear some space in a room and get stacking! Build a block tower as high as you can before it topples. Can you build a tower as tall as the ceiling? Take turns adding one block at a time until it falls over.

Challenge each other with a wooden stacking game such as Jenga or Ta-Ka-Radi. Make the tallest pyramid possible by stacking up paper or plastic cups. See if you can collapse the pyramid by blowing on the bottom layer.

Build a tower for your daughter's stuffed animals or dolls to live in. Cut windows and doors out of cardboard boxes, stack them, and hold them together with duct tape. Help your daughter decorate the tower with markers.

Make snack towers by layering crackers, cheese, lunch meat, and pickle slices into a stack. Do the same with a handful of sandwich cookies. Take turns eating the cookie off the top of the stack!

🌱 Grow

Have you ever climbed a high hill or observation tower, or enjoyed the view from the top of a high-rise building? You can see for a great distance from up there, can't you? Towers were a great way of defending forts and castles in the past—you could see your enemy coming from far away and be ready to defend yourselves.

In the Bible, Proverbs 18:10 tells us, "The name of the LORD is a fortified tower; the righteous run to it and are safe." God is our protection! He keeps watch over us and gives us safety in a world that is sometimes scary. Thank him for being your "tower" right now.

Dear Lord,

Thank you for loving us so much that you keep watch over us every day. Thank you for being our strong tower. You are mightier than anything that comes our way. Help us to trust you and run to you every time we are worried and afraid. Amen.

58

It's Beginning to Look a Lot Like Christmas

☞ Grab

» Christmas music
» Notebook and pencil
» Candy canes

» Car keys
» Money

Go

Christmas is a beautiful holiday—but it can be hectic. Enjoy this break in the activity to simply focus on your daughter. Grab your Christmas CDs and some candy canes, then hop in the car and begin your quest: to find the best holiday lights display in town!

Drive from neighborhood to neighborhood. Pull over to view the brightest, most colorful holiday light displays you see. Give the displays a grade, and note the locations of the A+ displays in your notebook in case you want to drive by and enjoy them another time.

When your tour of lights is over, stop for a hot cup of cocoa at a coffee shop.

❦ Grow

Share with your daughter about the best Christmas you ever had as a child. What was your most exciting gift? What traditions did your family keep from year to year? Which ones meant the most to you? Ask your daughter these questions:

» What is your all-time favorite Christmas carol?

    » What is your favorite Christmas tradition? Is it the tree? Visits from relatives? The stockings? A special treat your family always has? Christmas music on the radio? The special candlelight service at church?

    » What is the number-one gift on your wish list? Why?

At Christmastime we remember the most incredible gift ever: God sent his Son Jesus into the world as a baby so we could receive his gift of salvation. Read the following verses together:

> And God raised us up with Christ and seated us with him in the heavenly realms in Christ Jesus, in order that in the coming ages he might show the incomparable riches of his grace, expressed in his kindness to us in Christ Jesus. For it is by grace you have been saved, through faith—and this not from yourselves, it is the gift of God. (Eph. 2:6–8)

We are so blessed to have an entire holiday season devoted to praising God for his gift to us. Take some time to pray and thank him right now!

Dear Lord,

    Thank you for the Christmas season, when we celebrate how Jesus came into the world to save us. You have given us the most amazing gift we could ever imagine, and we'll be praising you for our salvation forever! Please show us how we can share the gift of your love with others. We need your wisdom to know how to best serve others and share what we have. Thank you again for Christmas. Amen!

59

Your Daughter's World

☞ Grab

» Decorative gift for your daughter's room
» Mini-picnic, such as fruit and crackers

Go

Dads, prepare to enter a strange and unfamiliar world—your daughter's room! Ask your daughter to prepare for your visit ahead of time. She can arrange all of the stuffed animals and dolls she'd like you to meet, and gather together the most recent drawings or crafts she's made. Perhaps she has a scrapbook, photo album, or school yearbook she'd like to look through with you. Make sure she has a favorite collection ready to show off, whether it's glass figurines, china dolls, hats, or a sticker album.

When she's ready for your visit, arrive at her bedroom door with a wrapped gift and snacks in hand. Knock politely and allow her to show you in! Sit on the floor and enjoy the window into her world. Ask questions about her toys, such as where she received them and what she likes about them. Take time to admire her artwork—be specific about what catches your eye in each one. If she has pictures of friends, take time to learn their names and hear her stories about them. Ooh and aah over her collections. Brainstorm about how you could add to her collection in the near future.

When your daughter has shared all of her special treasures with you, thank her for letting you visit. Enjoy your snack together and present her with the gift for her room.

❦ Grow

Romans 15:7 tells us that just like Christ has made us welcome, we should welcome one another into our lives. Today your daughter invited you into her room. She showed you her prized possessions—the things that reflect her unique personality and interests. Christ has also made us welcome. He made a way for us to have a home in heaven with him forever. Whenever you share your home or belongings with others, you are loving as Christ loves.

Dear Lord,

Thank you for making us welcome in the family of God. Thank you for the home you are preparing for us in heaven. We understand that you know us inside and out, and that our home in heaven will be perfect for us in every way. Please help us to be openhearted and willing to share our home and what we have with others. Please use our home as a blessing to all who come here. Thank you for my daughter and her willingness to share her room with me today. Help us to love each other as you love us, always. Amen.

60

Tell Me a Story

☞ Grab

» Timer or stopwatch
» Car keys
» Money

Go

Take a timer and your imaginations to your daughter's favorite ice cream shop. Get ready to create a wild story together! Choose a story opener, such as "Once upon a time there was a girl who loved ice cream. However, every time she ate some she became invisible!" Or, "Once upon a time there was a girl who loved ice cream so much, she decided to build her whole house out of it!" Decide who will begin the story, then set the timer for 45 seconds. Once the timer runs out, even if it's midsentence, trade roles and let the other person add to the story for 45 seconds. Continue taking turns with the story until you're ready for "The End." If you're having a great time, you can start over with a whole new story. And if you get stuck without ideas, just say, "And then the girl called her mother. Her mother said. . ."

> **Dad to Dad**
> *Check out "Rory's Story Cubes" by Gamewright for an alternative way to play a storytelling game.*

144

Grow

I'm sure your story took off in directions you never expected! The story's silly twists and turns are what make it so funny.

Would it have been as much fun to make up the story if only *one* of you was talking? Storytelling can be great practice in both speaking and listening. It was putting your separate ideas together that made the story entertaining. Sometimes we can get carried away with our own thoughts and take over a conversation. When we do that, we miss out on the great ideas of others and make them feel like they're unimportant.

The Bible says we should be "quick to listen [and] slow to speak" (James 1:19).

Proverbs 10:19 warns us, "Sin is unavoidable when there is much talk, but whoever seals his lips is wise" (GW). We have a wonderful promise in Proverbs 19:20: "Listen to advice and accept discipline, and at the end you will be counted among the wise." God knows best: we learn the most when our mouths are closed and our ears are open!

Dear Lord,

Thank you for this time to use our imaginations together. It is so fun to share our ideas and laugh. Thank you so much for offering us the gift of wisdom! Teach us the talent of listening so we don't miss out on what you want to teach us. Help us to memorize the verses we read so we can become quick to listen, slow to speak, and wise! Amen.

61

When Life Hands You Lemons . . .

☞ Grab

» Folding table
» Poster board and markers
» Instant lemonade mix or frozen concentrated lemonade
» Disposable cups
» Pitchers

» Small paper lunch sacks
» Microwave popcorn
» Cooler with ice
» Box or bag of coins to make change

Go

Is there anything better on a hot day than a lemonade stand? Be a team as you prepare one or two pitchers of lemonade, either from an instant mix or frozen concentrate. These two types also taste great when combined. Place pitchers in the refrigerator to cool. Pop some microwave popcorn and when it has cooled, fill paper sacks with the popcorn.

Meanwhile, create a sign for your lemonade stand. Decide on a price per cup of lemonade and bag of popcorn. Write on your sign with big, bold lettering to draw the attention of thirsty passersby. Encourage your daughter to add her own artwork to jazz up the sign.

Set up a folding table outside and attach your sign to the front. Be creative and think of ways to add interest to your table. Balloons? A tablecloth? A huge stuffed animal?

Bring out a cooler of ice, cups, your bag of coins, your pitchers of lemonade, and the bags of popcorn. Place one of the pitchers on the table and one in the cooler to stay cold. Let the sales begin!

Stick together outside, both for safety and to enjoy the experience as a team. Let your daughter do as much of the lemonade pouring and counting of change as possible. If sales are slow, enjoy some of the popcorn and lemonade yourselves!

> Dad's goal: to earn enough money to live-the same life as my wife and kids.
>
> Seen on a dad's T-shirt

When finished for the day, work together to clean up and put your supplies away. Count the money and see how much you earned from your business. Decide how you will use the earnings: half to give away and half to save for fun another day?

🌱 Grow

Was it fun to make snacks and sell them in your neighborhood? Were you happy with how much you were able to earn? You worked hard to prepare your stand and keep it going outside. It's always great when hard work pays off.

You probably would have had some unhappy customers if you had sold either sugar water or lemon juice, though. It's the combination of sweet and sour that makes lemonade so delicious. That's a little bit like life—sometimes things are "sweet" and going smoothly, but other times are "sour" with stress and difficulty. The good and the bad combined teach us a lot about God and grow our faith. James 1:2–4 reminds us:

> Consider it pure joy, my brothers and sisters, whenever you face trials of many kinds, because you know that the testing of your faith produces perseverance. Let perseverance finish its work so that you may be mature and complete, not lacking anything.

I know *I* don't want to be lacking anything good that God has for me. Bring on the lemons!

Dear Lord,

Thank you for our fun time making a lemonade stand today. And thank you for sometimes allowing hard things to happen to us. We know you will use every trial to teach us and make us more like Jesus. Help us to hold tight to your promise in Romans 8:28: "And we know that in all things God works for the good of those who love him, who have been called according to his purpose." Thank you for making our "lemons" into lemonade—we love you! Amen.

62

Have a Ball

☞ Grab

» Clothing in your team's colors   » Car keys
» Money

Go

Whether it's a nationally televised pro football game or a basketball game at your local high school, nothing beats the fun of cheering on your favorite team!

Gear up in your team colors. If you're feeling bold, bring out the face paint and foam fingers! Travel to the stadium, field, or gym of the sporting event. Grab your seats and check out the action around you. How are they prepping the field? Are there players and cheerleaders warming up? Once the game begins, be sure to point out your favorite players and explain the rules and calls by the refs to your daughter—or ask her to explain them to you. And of course, don't forget the hot dogs!

🌱 Grow

In every game there's a winner and a loser. How do you think the winning team is feeling right now? How about the losing team? Do you think that one person on the team gets all the credit for winning the game? Does one person get all the blame for their team's loss? Sometimes one person has an amazing pass or goal, or one person makes a crazy mistake, but usually it takes great teamwork to win and poor teamwork to lose.

Families are like that too. We have to be a team to have a happy home. If only one person is doing all the chores, they're going to feel overworked and stressed out. If one person oversleeps, it makes everybody late to church on Sunday morning. Everybody needs to be pitching in and helping each other out for things to go smoothly.

What are some ways our family works together so our home can "win"?

When have things been hard at home because somebody "fouled" and let the others down?

Read these verses together:

> How good and pleasant it is
> when God's people live together in unity! (Ps. 133:1)

As holy people whom God has chosen and loved, be sympathetic, kind, humble, gentle, and patient. Put up with each other, and forgive each other if anyone has a complaint. Forgive as the Lord forgave you. Above all, be loving. This ties everything together perfectly. (Col. 3:12–14 GW)

What a great blueprint for a family: we put up with each other's weaknesses, care about each other's struggles, and forgive. It's our love for each other that keeps us on the same team!

Dear God,

Please let us be the kind of family that "dwells in unity." Help us to be a team by helping each other out and cheering each other on. Sometimes we do let each other down. Please enable us to show forgiveness every time. Teach us to care for each other the way you do, with patience and perfect love. Amen!

63

Rise and Shine

☞ Grab

» Money
» Car keys
» Alarm clock

Go

The night before, check your local forecast for the time of the next day's sunrise. Set your alarm a little earlier than this so you'll be up before the sun.

In the morning, wake up your daughter and head to a local donut shop. (Don't wake up the rest of your sleepy family as you head out the door!) Pick out a favorite muffin or donut and take it to-go. Drive together to a spot with a great view to watch the sunrise.

As you sit and enjoy your breakfast, enjoy the light as it begins to fill the sky. Take note of which colors you see in the clouds and when you see the edge of the sun first appear above the horizon. Celebrate a beautiful new day!

☙ Grow

Every morning is really a miracle. It's a fresh new day full of possibilities. The best part is that each morning begins one more day in which we can see how God loves us through everything that happens.

The steadfast love of the LORD never ceases;
his mercies never come to an end;
they are new every morning;
great is your faithfulness. (Lam. 3:22–23 ESV)

» How did we see God show his love for us yesterday?
» Did anything happen yesterday that you wish you could do over?

Today is a day of second chances. We can be a better friend, have a more thankful heart, and work hard to learn something new. It's exciting that God will be walking beside us all through this day, ready to help us every minute.

Dear God,

Thank you for this beautiful morning and the exciting possibilities that this day holds. Please help us to count our blessings today. Fill our hearts with love and kindness for everyone we see. Help us to be brave when hard things happen. Most of all, give us eyes to see how real you are and how you're with us all the time. We love you! Amen.

64

Play with Clay

☞ Grab

» Tub of white air-dry clay or reservations at a pottery studio

» Washable paints, brushes
» Miscellaneous clay-carving tools

Go

Roll up your sleeves and get ready to create a masterpiece! If you're making your clay creations at home, clear a workspace on a table or countertop. Begin working a small piece of clay in your hands until it softens. Take your clay and use the tools you have at hand to form animals, miniature plates of food, tiles, ornaments, bowls, or whatever else you can dream up. Roll the clay into a long rope and coil it to form a small jar or pot. Moisten your fingertips with water and smooth out the clay with your fingers. Use toothpicks or other tools to carve letters or a design into the soft clay. Roll out a piece with a small, smooth drinking glass and use cookie cutters to cut out various shapes. The end of a straw is useful for imprinting circles or cutting out a small hole to hang the artwork from once it's dry.

Place your finished pieces on a tray covered with wax paper. Place the tray in an out-of-the-way spot until the pieces have dried. (Remember, larger, thicker pieces will take longer to dry than small, thin ones.) Once the pieces have hardened, have a great time adding color with paint.

If you're decorating clay items at a pottery studio, have fun choosing from the pieces available. Allow the staff to guide you as you select and create your artwork. Set a time to return to the studio to pick up your kiln-fired pieces. Display your daughter's amazing creations for everyone to enjoy!

❦ Grow

Sometimes God is described as a potter. This is because just like you used your imaginations to create clay figures, God used his imagination to create you and me!

> Yet you, LORD, are our Father.
> We are the clay, you are the potter;
> we are all the work of your hand. (Isa. 64:8)

Ask your daughter these questions:

» Did the clay argue with you about what it wanted to be?

» Do you ever wish you could look like someone else?

» Do you ever wish you had a different personality or talents than you do?

» Do you ever get frustrated with yourself when you make a mistake?

Sometimes we wish we could have a makeover or a "do-over" with our life. We'd like to be better looking, more talented, a better student, or more popular. When it comes down to it, we sometimes think we're just a big mistake! The Bible challenges this kind of thinking in Romans 9:20:

> But who are you, a human being, to talk back to God? "Shall what is formed say to the one who formed it, 'Why did you make me like this?'"

When we wish we could be someone else, we're really telling God that he made a mistake when he made us this way. Take a few minutes to write a list of the things that make you unique and special, both inside and out.

Dear Father,

Thank you for being the potter that made us! Help us to trust your wisdom for making us the way we are. Please forgive us for the times we complain and put ourselves down. You have an awesome imagination. We thank you for loving us so much that you made each of us one-of-a-kind. You know us better than anyone, and you love us no matter what! Amen.

65

All Dressed Up and Someplace to Go

☞ Grab

» Money   » Camera

» Car keys

Go

Your daughter may be rough-and-tumble or as feminine as they come. Regardless, sometimes a girl needs a really beautiful dress for a holiday or other special occasion. Nobody is better than a dad at making a daughter feel like a princess!

Escort your daughter to a local clothing or department store. Choose a variety of dresses from the racks and have your daughter try them on in the dressing room. Make sure she models each one so you can "ooh and aah" and take her picture. Veto any choices that don't fit well or are immodest. Have her set her favorites to the side in a "maybe pile." If she doesn't care for any of them, take the time to shop at other stores until you find *the one*.

Take a look at each dress in the maybe pile. Take a look at the photos in your digital camera as well. Narrow the choices down by having your daughter eliminate one at a time until you have a final decision.

You may have shopped till you dropped, but your daughter will think of her time with you whenever she wears her beautiful new dress.

> **Dad to Dad**
>
> *For some great tips for girls about dressing with modesty, check out Dannah Gresh's "Truth or Bare" fashion test with your daughter at www. secretkeepergirl.com!*

🌾 Grow

Choosing a new dress is one way you're getting ready for a special day. Taking the time to look your best and putting on something different from the ordinary makes it even more memorable.

God made his girls to be beautiful on the outside *and* the inside:

> Watching your daughter being collected by her date feels like handing over a million-dollar Stradivarius to a gorilla.
>
> **Jim Bishop**

> Beauty doesn't come from hairstyles, gold jewelry, or clothes. Rather, beauty is something internal that can't be destroyed. Beauty expresses itself in a gentle and quiet attitude which God considers precious. (1 Pet. 3:3–4 GW)

God is different from the rest of us:

> The LORD does not look at the things people look at. People look at the outward appearance, but the LORD looks at the heart. (1 Sam. 16:7)

Even when we're having a "bad hair day" or our clothes are out of style, God is looking at how we love him and each other. Let's enjoy "dressing up" our hearts with his kind of beauty!

Dear Father,

Thank you for my beautiful girl. Not only is she wonderful to look at on the outside, she has a sweet spirit and kindness that make her shine! Please protect her mind from believing that her worth is found in her looks. Help her to care more about her heart attitudes than her outfits. May the dress we found today bring a smile whenever she wears it—we'll be remembering her heart and her inner beauty! We love you. Amen.

66

What Do You *Do* All Day?

☞ Grab

> » Camera
> » Money
> » Car keys

Go

Are you ready to invite your daughter into your work world? Make sure she has everything necessary, such as a hard hat, safety goggles, or security pass if your workplace requires it. Check with your supervisor for prior approval of her visit. Team up to pack your lunches (or at least a snack) and head to work!

Walk your daughter through a regular day at your place of business. Do you punch a time clock? Log into a computer system? Fill out a daily report? Show her your individual workspace and all of your equipment and supplies. Introduce her to your supervisor and co-workers too. Give her a tour of the facility so she can see the places like the file room, warehouse, and lunchroom. Share something with her that she can keep, such as a company calendar, business card, or an item printed with the company logo. Take a break and enjoy your snack or lunch together. Have her take a picture of you in your work area so she can visualize you during the day when you're apart.

✿ Grow

Sometimes work is, well, work! But it is also a gift from God because it is one of the ways he provides for our needs. If daddies didn't go to work it would be hard to buy groceries or gas for the car. Let your daughter "interview" you with the following questions:

» What are some of the most fun parts of your job?

» Which parts of your job are the most challenging?

» Did you have to go to school or train for your type of work?

» As a kid, what did you want to be when you grew up?

» What was the first job you ever had?

No matter what job we have, God wants us to work hard with a willing attitude. That's because our *real* boss is God, and we should do our work to please him more than anybody else.

Whatever you do, work at it with all your heart, as working for the Lord, not for human masters, since you know that you will receive an inheritance from the Lord as a reward. It is the Lord Christ you are serving. (Col. 3:23–24)

Dear Lord,

Thank you for giving Dad a job that provides for our family. Please help him work with a cheerful heart and a helpful attitude toward the people he works with. Please increase his talents and give him a good reputation for being a faithful worker. Thank you for the work you have planned for each of us in the future. You are so good! Amen!

67

An Apple a Day . . .

☛ Grab

- » Fall jackets and boots
- » Camera
- » Money
- » Car keys

Go

Check your local classifieds to find a u-pick apple orchard with hay rides. Dress for the cool autumn weather and enjoy your drive in the country as you make your way to the farm.

Grab the bags or buckets the orchard provides and make your way out to the apple trees. Select your favorite apple varieties and get picking! Give your daughter a boost if she sees a big, beautiful piece of fruit that she can't reach.

When you've picked enough to snack on (and make a pie or two!), enjoy everything the orchard has to offer. Perhaps you'll find pumpkins, some hot apple cider, and even some gourds or a scarecrow. Take time for an old-fashioned ride on a hay wagon. Make the most of every photo opportunity!

When you're finished with your amazing autumn experience, spend some time in the Word and pray together.

🌱 Grow

Autumn is a time to celebrate the harvest after a long summer of hard work. It's a thrill to look around and see God's goodness in the way he has provided food for the coming seasons. Isn't it amazing that only a few months ago the apples in your hands were just little buds on a tree?

One thing is for certain: apple trees bring a harvest of apples, lemon trees produce lemons, and peach trees grow peaches! God says that there will be a "harvest" in people, too, depending on what has been planted.

> A man reaps what he sows. Whoever sows to please their flesh, from the flesh will reap destruction; whoever sows to please the Spirit, from the Spirit will reap eternal life. Let us not become weary in doing good, for at the proper time we will reap a harvest if we do not give up. Therefore, as we have opportunity, let us do good to all people, especially to those who belong to the family of believers. (Gal. 6:7–10)

James 3:18 also teaches us this: "Peacemakers who sow in peace reap a harvest of righteousness."

» Make a list of "seeds" you can plant to please the Spirit of God.

» Make a list of ways you can "do good to all people." How can you serve and care for others?

» Make another list of ways you can be a peacemaker in your home, church, school, and workplace.

When we are loving and caring toward others, and when we do all we can to get along with one another, God fills us with more and more of the love of Jesus. And righteousness is a better harvest than apples any day!

Dear Lord,

Please plant your love in our hearts! We want a harvest of goodness, peace, and love. Teach us how to serve other people. Help us make peace with everyone around us. Let us not water any "seeds" of sin that might be growing in the soil of our hearts. Sometimes doing the right thing can be tough—give us strength to never give up. Thank you for the promise of a life forever with you. We love you! Amen.

68

Around the World in 80 Minutes

☞ Grab

» Your appetite   » Car keys
» Money

Go

Today you're going to travel around the world! Well, at least your taste buds are. Drive to a nearby Asian restaurant and order an egg roll, wontons, or a couple of dumplings. Enjoy the snack, and then take a moment to pray for the nation that the restaurant represents. For example, "Dear Lord, thank you for our Christian brothers and sisters in China. Please protect them and keep them close to you. Please give them the freedom to worship you, and may their witness lead many to salvation. Amen."

Continue visiting a variety of restaurants with international fare. Grab a burrito from a Mexican restaurant, for example, or find a French baguette or croissant, some Indian naan bread, American potato chips, a slice of pizza or Italian gelato, a dish of German potato salad, a slice of Swiss cheese, or Chilean grapes. Briefly pray for the salvation and freedom of worship for the citizens of each country you "taste."

> **Dad to Dad**
> Check out www.kidsofcourage.com with your daughter to learn how children around the world are living for Jesus and sharing the message of salvation.

✿ Grow

We are so blessed to have the freedom to worship God. So many people around the world don't have the freedom we experience every day. Would it be hard if we had to keep our faith in God a secret? What would it be like if we weren't allowed to have a Bible at home? Can you imagine not being allowed to go to church on Sunday?

It is exciting to imagine that wonderful day in the future when Jesus will bring all of his people to heaven to be with him. He says that:

> At the name of Jesus every knee should bow, in heaven and on earth and under the earth, and every tongue confess that Jesus Christ is Lord, to the glory of God the Father. (Phil. 2:10–11)

What an incredible moment it will be when every believer in the world, from every tribe and nation, will gather in one place to praise God together!

Dear God,

Thank you for the hope we have of being in heaven with you. Please protect our Christian brothers and sisters around the world who follow you no matter how dangerous it might be. Give us the courage to stand up for you no matter what. Thank you that someday we can worship you with all of the believers in the world in total freedom. Come soon! Amen.

69

"Sticking" Together

☞ Grab

> » Rolls of duct tape in various colors
> » Your imagination!

Go

Brainstorm about what you'd like to make with your duct tape. A limitless number of ideas can be found online (try www.duckbrand.com or www.thriftyfun.com) including wallets, video game covers, bracelets, animals, flowers, costumes, and so on. A favorite at our house is covering empty tissue boxes with duct tape. These boxes can hold all of your daughter's little notes, toys, or stickers that she enjoys collecting. You can also use various colors of tape to cover or embellish an old backpack or purse.

☖ Grow

Duct tape has been used for a countless number of purposes, from repairing the Apollo 13 lunar module and saving the astronauts' lives to fixing helicopter rotors in the Vietnam War. It can be used to cure warts, make prom dresses, and fix your car. It's cool how something so fun to play with can be useful too.

Just like duct tape can come in handy as a fix-it in so many situations, the Word of God is a blessing to us in everything that ever happens in our lives. Are you confused and don't know what to do?

All Scripture is God-breathed and is useful for teaching, rebuking, correcting and training in righteousness, so that the servant of God may be thoroughly equipped for every good work. (2 Tim. 3:16–17)

Are you feeling worried or afraid?

> You are my refuge and my shield;
> I have put my hope in your word. (Ps. 119:114)

Do you have a reason to celebrate and praise God?

Let the message of Christ dwell among you richly as you teach and admonish one another with all wisdom through psalms, hymns, and songs from the Spirit, singing to God with gratitude in your hearts. (Col. 3:16)

Whether you're sad, angry, worried, or happy, the Bible is filled with words of hope and praise. Pray these verses from Psalm 119 together to thank God for his gift of the Scriptures:

> Blessed are those whose ways are blameless,
> who walk according to the law of the LORD.
> Blessed are they who keep his statutes
> and seek him with all their heart—
> they do no wrong
> but follow his ways. (vv. 1–3)
>
> I seek you with all my heart;
> do not let me stray from your commands.
> I have hidden your word in my heart
> that I might not sin against you.
> Praise be to you, O LORD;
> teach me your decrees.
> With my lips I recount
> all the laws that come from your mouth.
> I rejoice in following your statutes
> as one rejoices in great riches.
> I meditate on your precepts
> and consider your ways.

I delight in your decrees;
I will not neglect your word. (vv. 10–16)

Your word, LORD, is eternal;
it stands firm in the heavens.
Your faithfulness continues through all generations;
you established the earth, and it endures.
Your laws endure to this day,
for all things serve you. (vv. 89–91)

How sweet are your words to my taste,
sweeter than honey to my mouth!
I gain understanding from your precepts;
therefore I hate every wrong path.
Your word is a lamp for my feet,
a light on my path. (vv. 103–5)

Amen!

70

Put Your Heart into It!

☞ Grab

- » Valentine's Day conversation heart candies
- » Computer and printer
- » Small, heart-shaped box of chocolates
- » Pink carnation
- » Valentine's Day greeting card
- » Money
- » Car keys

Go

Love is in the air on Valentine's Day! Find printable Valentine's bingo pages online at websites such as dltk-kids.com, making friends.com, or Crayola.com. Print out a few bingo pages and use conversation heart candies as game markers. Have your daughter dress for the occasion in holiday colors such as red, pink, or purple.

At the beginning of your date, present your daughter with a box of chocolates, a pink carnation, and a Valentine's Day greeting card. Take her, along with the bingo game and heart candies, to an ice cream parlor. Order an ice cream sundae to share and play a few bingo games together. Flip the bingo pages over and draw tic-tac-toe grids and hangman games on the back. Use the conversation hearts as your tic-tac-toe markers and come up with Valentine's-themed words to guess for hangman. End the date with a hug and an "I love you!"

Dad to Dad

Dads, this is a good date during the month of February, but save the actual holiday to romance your wife! Enlist your daughter's help in thinking up special gift and restaurant ideas to express your love for your bride.

🌱 Grow

On Valentine's Day we show our love in so many ways—gifts, flowers, candy, and fun memories together. While we take a day to remember how much we love each other, we can also remember how very much our Father in heaven loves us! Read these verses together:

> He didn't tell me how to live; he lived, and let me watch him do it.
>
> Clarence Budington Kelland

And I pray that you, being rooted and established in love, may have power, together with all the Lord's holy people, to grasp how wide and long and high and deep is the love of Christ, and to know this love that surpasses knowledge—that you may be filled to the measure of all the fullness of God. (Eph. 3:17–19)

Dear friends, let us love one another, for love comes from God. Everyone who loves has been born of God and knows God. Whoever does not love does not know God, because God is love. This is how God showed his love among us: He sent his one and only Son into the world that we might live through him. This is love: not that we loved God, but that he loved us and sent his Son as an atoning sacrifice for our sins. Dear friends, since God so loved us, we also ought to love one another. No one has ever seen God; but if we love one another, God lives in us and his love is made complete in us. (1 John 4:7–12)

Dear Lord,

Thank you for your love that is "wide and long and high and deep." Help us to know it! And please give us love for one another because you have loved us first. Thank you for this great day to express our love for each other. Please help us to show it every day of the year. Amen!

71

Count Your Blessings

☞ Grab

- » Index cards
- » Markers
- » Scissors
- » Money
- » Car keys

Go

I'm sure at Thanksgiving you're thankful for . . . pie! Take your daughter to a favorite restaurant and order a big slice for each of you. Cut twenty index cards in half to make forty smaller cards. Talk together and think of twenty people or things you are thankful for. Use markers to write down or draw a picture of each blessing on two of the cards, making twenty matching pairs. Shuffle the cards together and lay them facedown in rows on the table. Take turns flipping two cards over at a time as you play Thanksgiving Memory. If the cards you pick up don't match, place them facedown again. When one of you picks up two cards that match, keep the pair and set them to the side. When all of the cards have been matched, see who has collected the most pairs!

ᚐᚉ Grow

Thanksgiving is a fantastic holiday because it's simple: family, food, and football. What could be better for our spirits than taking a day to remember how blessed we are? You probably could have filled stacks and stacks of index cards with things to be thankful for.

When we take the time to remember how good our God really is, we're following the example of believers through all of history (even before the Pilgrims!). Read these verses together:

> Give thanks to the LORD, for he is good;
> his love endures forever. (Ps. 118:29)

Through Jesus, therefore, let us continually offer to God a sacrifice of praise—the fruit of lips that confess his name. (Heb. 13:15)

> Shout for joy to the LORD, all the earth.
> Worship the LORD with gladness;
> come before him with joyful songs.
> Know that the LORD is God.
> It is he who made us, and we are his;
> we are his people, the sheep of his pasture.
>
> Enter his gates with thanksgiving
> and his courts with praise;
> give thanks to him and praise his name.
> For the LORD is good and his love endures forever;
> his faithfulness continues through all generations. (Ps. 100)

Dear Father,

Your gifts to us are too many to count. Give us thankful hearts that never stop praising you! Please help us to make every day a Thanksgiving Day, for you are good and your love endures forever! Amen.

72

It's Out of This World

☛ Grab

» Money
» Car keys

Go

Check out the location of a public planetarium in or near your community. Give the facility a call to find out the schedule of events and plan your visit. Keep the weather forecast in mind; a cloudy night will interfere with stargazing!

Bring your daughter to the planetarium and take advantage of each available exhibit.

> **Dad to Dad**
>
> *To really appreciate the awe-inspiring hand of God in the universe, watch these videos with your daughter: "Indescribable" and "How Great is Our God" by Louie Giglio, and "The Star of Bethlehem" by Rick Larson.*

ᛉ Grow

Staring up at the huge expanse of space can be a powerful experience! Did you know that our sun is so big it could hold 1,300,000 of our earths? And that our sun is just one of 100 billion stars in our galaxy? And that our galaxy is one of at least 100 billion galaxies in the universe—that we know of? The size of the universe is too big to even imagine.

What's amazing is that our God is so big he created the entire universe himself. Every time we look at the stars in the sky it should cause our hearts to worship him! Read these verses together:

> The heavens declare the glory of God;
> the skies proclaim the work of his hands.
> Day after day they pour forth speech;
> night after night they reveal knowledge.
> They have no speech, they use no words;
> no sound is heard from them.
> Yet their voice goes out into all the earth,
> their words to the ends of the world. (Ps. 19:1–4)

10 Things Your Daughter Needs from You

1. Point her to Jesus—help her build her life on solid ground.
2. Unconditional love—let her know you'll love her no matter what.
3. Prayers—for her emotional, physical, and spiritual growth and protection.
4. Love her mom—if you love, respect, and cherish your wife, your daughter will learn what it means to be loved.
5. Affection—hugs from dad are important!
6. Faithfulness—she needs you to be the one man in her life she can depend on completely.
7. Affirmation—give her praise, kudos, way-to-gos, high fives, pats on the back. Did I mention your daughter needs you to affirm her?
8. Memories—give her special experiences with you that she'll remember for a lifetime.
9. Character—your integrity, honesty, courage, and kindness will show her what a good man really is.
10. Leadership—be a man that protects and guides your family well.

You alone are the LORD. You made the heavens, even the highest heavens, and all their starry host, the earth and all that is on it, the seas and all that is in them. You give life to everything, and the multitudes of heaven worship you. (Neh. 9:6)

> For as high as the heavens are above the earth,
> so great is his love for those who fear him. (Ps. 103:11)

Dear Lord,

Thank you for making everything in the universe. You are brilliant! Help us to praise you whenever we look up at the awesome night sky. We love you so much. Amen.

73

What's Bugging You?

☞ Grab

» Clean, empty glass jars
» Butterfly net

» Old white sheet or umbrella
» Insect field guide

Go

Today you and your daughter can explore the smaller things in life: bugs! Create a beat sheet in your backyard by spreading an old sheet or umbrella beneath some bushes. Shake the plants and see which insects fall onto your beat sheet. Put them in your collection jars to get a closer look before releasing them into the yard again.

If there is a flat, moist area in your yard you may be able to find some earthworms! Try lifting up rocks or logs to see what small creatures may be living underneath. Keep in mind that larger rocks may be a habitat for less-than-friendly wildlife such as snakes or spiders, so be cautious.

Later in the evening, a light trap can be used to attract a variety of insects. Hang a white sheet behind your porch light or shine a light onto a white garage door. Bugs will be attracted to the white surface and you will be able to catch them for a good look before setting them free.

🌱 Grow

Every living thing, big or small, lives in its own unique habitat. When God created the world he knew exactly which home would suit each living thing. If you collected any bugs during your date, you knew that they wouldn't thrive for long if they were kept in the jars instead of living free where they belong.

We have an ideal spiritual "habitat" as well. God knows we need to be fed by the Word, drink the "living water" Jesus brings, and live our lives alongside other followers of Christ. Read these verses together:

> Then Jesus declared, "I am the bread of life. Whoever comes to me will never go hungry, and whoever believes in me will never be thirsty." (John 6:35)

> And let us consider how we may spur one another on toward love and good deeds, not giving up meeting together, as some are in the habit of doing, but encouraging one another—and all the more as you see the Day approaching. (Heb. 10:24–25)

> His divine power has given us everything we need for a godly life through our knowledge of him who called us by his own glory and goodness. (2 Pet. 1:3)

Dear Father,

Thank you for giving us a place where we belong: in your kingdom! Help us to know the Bible, to pray with you about everything, and to stay close to other believers who can encourage us. Thank you for giving us everything that we need! Amen.

74

Twenty Questions

☞ Grab

» Two paper grocery sacks
» Hammer
» Can of soup

» Box of tissues
» New stuffed animal

Go

Is this another date? Will it be fun? It's Twenty Questions! Place all of the items you gathered into a paper sack and fold the top closed. Instruct your daughter to find three items of her choice to place in her own paper bag.

Begin the date by choosing a place to go for ice cream, but keep it to yourself! Have your daughter guess where you're going by asking you questions. Do they have fast food? Have we been there before? Once she figures out where you're going, head on over there with your bags in hand.

Once you're seated and have ordered your dessert, challenge your daughter to guess what your bag contains, beginning with the hammer. Only respond to yes or no questions, such as "Is it metal?" or "Can I eat it?" Open-ended questions like "What color is it?" just won't work. When (or if) your daughter guesses that it's a hammer, show it to her before closing up the bag again. Now it's your turn to guess the first item in her bag.

Take turns playing Twenty Questions and see if you can guess what you each placed in your bags. Save the stuffed animal for last and make it her prize for finishing the game.

⚘ Grow

It's fun and easy to play a game of Twenty Questions. It's a lot more difficult when we try to answer the questions of life: Why do bad things happen to people? Why hasn't God answered my prayer yet? When will Jesus come back? It's good to know that God doesn't mind our questions. He's ready to help us when we're discouraged or filled with doubt.

Read David's prayers in the Bible when he was wrestling with hard questions:

> How long, LORD? Will you forget me forever?
> How long will you hide your face from me?
> How long must I wrestle with my thoughts
> and day after day have sorrow in my heart?
> How long will my enemy triumph over me? (Ps. 13:1–2)

> As the deer pants for streams of water,
> so my soul pants for you, my God.
> My soul thirsts for God, for the living God.
> When can I go and meet with God?
> My tears have been my food
> day and night,
> while people say to me all day long,
> "Where is your God?" (Ps. 42:1–3)

God won't leave us hanging—he wants us to discover how real he is and how eager he is to meet our needs. He promises to meet us in the middle of our doubts and questions. Read his promise in Matthew 7:7–11:

> Ask and it will be given to you; seek and you will find; knock and the door will be opened to you. For everyone who asks receives;

the one who seeks finds; and to the one who knocks, the door will be opened.

Which of you, if your son asks for bread, will give him a stone? Or if he asks for a fish, will give him a snake? If you, then, though you are evil, know how to give good gifts to your children, how much more will your Father in heaven give good gifts to those who ask him!

Dear Father,

Thank you for your patience with us when we have doubts and questions. Thank you for hearing our prayers. We know you care about every struggle we face. You know when we worry or don't have what we need. Give us faith to trust in your goodness so we don't lose heart. Teach us to wait for you with confidence. You will always meet us in the middle of our situation. We love you! Amen.

75

Dinner and a Show

☞ Grab

» Money
» Car keys

Go

Check your local restaurant listings and reviews to find a good hibachi-style restaurant near you. Call ahead in case reservations are needed. Travel with your daughter to the restaurant and read through the menu together.

After you place your order, encourage your daughter to be adventurous as she tries Asian soup, tea, and maybe even chopsticks for the first time. Enjoy the show as the chef slices, dices, and tosses your dinner together with flair!

Grow

It's likely you have had rice, vegetables, and meat on your dinner plate many times in the past. What made this meal different, however, was the dramatic way it was prepared. It's entertaining to see the flames from the grill and the flashing knives of the chef right in front of you!

Sometimes we feel as if our days are repetitive and predictable. It's the same old "rice-and-vegetables" every day. How can we change our point of view so we are excited about each new morning? How does God give our lives meaning? Read Paul's words to the Colossians. Write down the words in bold print to make a list of the gifts we've been given.

> For this reason, since the day we heard about you, we have not stopped praying for you. We continually ask God to fill you with the **knowledge of his will** through all the **wisdom** and **understanding** that the Spirit gives, so that you may live a **life worthy of the Lord** and please him in every way: bearing fruit in **every good work**, growing in the **knowledge of God**, being strengthened with **all power** according to his glorious might so that you may have great **endurance** and **patience**, and giving joyful thanks to the Father, who has qualified you to share in the **inheritance of his holy people** in the kingdom of light. For he has **rescued us** from the dominion of darkness and brought us into the **kingdom of the Son** he loves, in whom we have **redemption**, the **forgiveness of sins**. (Col. 1:9–14)

With gifts like that from God, how could each day *not* be amazing! With his wisdom, good work to do, knowledge and power, and the hope of the kingdom of the Son, our days are filled with promise.

Dear God,

Thank you that when we belong to you, there is no "ordinary" day. We are so excited about the wisdom, power, knowledge, and inheritance you have for us. Teach us to use these gifts to do good work for you. Help us to keep our joy—we have so much to look forward to! Thank you for bringing us into your kingdom. Amen.

76

Rock, Paper, Scissors

☞ Grab

» Construction paper
» Scissors
» Markers

» Money
» Car keys

Go

Cut a piece of blue construction paper into six pieces. Use markers to write the name of a fun activity on each of the pieces, such as bowling, biking, playing at the park, swimming, playing mini-golf, or playing a video game.

Cut a piece of green construction paper into six pieces. On each piece write the name of a small gift like stickers, pencils, candy, nail polish, jewelry, or a notebook.

Cut a piece of red construction paper into six pieces. Write the names of different places to go for dessert or a snack on each piece.

Fold the pieces of construction paper so you can't see what is written on them. Start with the blue pieces of paper. Play Rock, Paper, Scissors. Whoever wins two out of three gets to draw one of the blue pieces of paper to name your activity choice for the day.

Repeat this game with the green papers to choose a small gift to purchase for your daughter. Then play the game with the red pieces of paper to decide where you will go for a treat on your date.

Get in the car and go have a great time playing together. Stop at a store to pick out the gift that was chosen for your daughter.

Wrap up your time together with a treat or a snack before heading home.

〽 Grow

No matter which activity, gift, and treat you ended up with, it was bound to be a great combo for a wonderful time together! Don't you wish you could make all your decisions just by playing Rock, Paper, Scissors? How do we know what to do when we have tough choices to make?

God promises that if we need wisdom we just have to ask him and he'll come through.

> If any of you lacks wisdom, you should ask God, who gives generously to all without finding fault, and it will be given to you. (James 1:5)

> I instruct you in the way of wisdom
> and lead you along straight paths.
> When you walk, your steps will not be
> hampered;
> when you run, you will not stumble.
> Hold on to instruction, do not let it go;
> guard it well, for it is your life. (Prov. 4:11–13)

> Every girl wants to believe that she is captivating, worth fighting for. She wants to know . . . Am I Lovely? Only you, Dad, can answer those questions. That makes you the most powerful man in your child's life.
>
> John Eldredge, *You Have What It Takes: What Every Father Needs to Know*

Dear Father,

We're so glad that you are in control—we don't have to be afraid of an uncertain future. Thank you for your promise to give us wisdom when we need it. Teach us to come to you with our tough choices. We know you will guide us and help us by your Spirit. Most of all, give us hearts that want to do your will and live for you. You are good! Amen.

77

Nutcracker Ballet

☞ Grab

» Ballet tickets
» Semi-formal clothing

Go

Pre-purchase tickets for a production of the *Nutcracker* ballet. To build anticipation for the ballet performance, listen to the music of Tchaikovsky's *Nutcracker Suite* before you go. Find a picture book of the *Nutcracker* to read together so your daughter is familiar with the storyline.

On the evening of the performance, admire your daughter all dressed up! Make your way to the theater and read the program together while you're waiting for the curtain to rise.

Enjoy watching the story of Clara and her nutcracker unfold before you.

✿ Grow

It's always a thrill to watch good triumph over evil. Great stories have the hero coming out on top. In fairy tales, the big bad wolf always loses and the special girl always wins the prince's heart. In the Nutcracker, it's exciting to see the defeat of the mouse king! Thankfully this doesn't just happen in stories: God gives us victory in our battle with sin and temptation every day!

Ask each other these questions:

» Can you name three temptations that you "battle" every day?

» What helps you to stand strong and do the right thing?

» What mistakes do we make that allow temptation to win the fight?

The Bible gives us encouragement when we struggle to do what is right:

> No temptation has overtaken you except what is common to mankind. And God is faithful; he will not let you be tempted beyond what you can bear. But when you are tempted, he will also provide a way out so that you can endure it. (1 Cor. 10:13)

> He will also keep you firm to the end, so that you will be blameless on the day of our Lord Jesus Christ. God is faithful, who has called you into fellowship with his Son, Jesus Christ our Lord. (1 Cor. 1:8–9)

Dear Lord,

Thank you for being our hero. You set us free from the power of sin! Thank you that you are ready to help us stand strong against any temptation that comes our way. Thank you for your promise to always give us a way to escape. Give us hearts that want to please you by living for you in every way. When we do give in to temptation, help us to run to you for forgiveness and a fresh start. We love you! Amen.

78

How I Met Your Mother

☞ Grab

» Your wedding photo album
» Your wedding video
» Car keys
» Money

Go

Every girl appreciates a good love story. Today you can share with your daughter how you met her mom and became a family. Describe where you were when you met, what you did on your first date, when you knew she was "the one," and how you proposed. Share with her about how you chose the engagement ring and if you had to ask for Grandpa's permission to marry his daughter. Flip through your wedding photo album together and watch your wedding video.

Take your daughter to the store so she can help choose a fresh bouquet of flowers for Mom. Tell her that just like her mom carried flowers on her wedding day, she deserves to have flowers right now because you still love her!

Grow

God created the idea of marriage and family. He says that a husband and wife are a living, walking picture of how the church honors God and how Jesus loves the church: completely and forever!

Husbands, love your wives, just as Christ loved the church and gave himself up for her to make her holy, cleansing her by the washing with water through the word, and to present her to himself as a radiant church, without stain or wrinkle or any other blemish, but holy and blameless. In this same way, husbands ought to love their wives as their own bodies. He who loves his wife loves himself. (Eph. 5:25–28)

Love isn't just a warm fuzzy feeling. First Corinthians 13:4–8 tells us what true love looks like:

Love is patient, love is kind. It does not envy, it does not boast, it is not proud. It does not dishonor others, it is not self-seeking, it is not easily angered, it keeps no record of wrongs. Love does not delight in evil but rejoices with the truth. It always protects, always trusts, always hopes, always perseveres. Love never fails.

It's an amazing gift to be loved like this!

Dear Father,

Thank you for loving us so perfectly. Please teach us to love like you do. Thank you for giving me a wife that blesses me so much. Thank you for making us a family and giving us a beautiful daughter to share our love. Keep us close to you and close to each other. Amen!

79

A Doggone Great Date

☞ Grab

» Tickets to an AKC dog show
» Car keys

Go

Check out the schedule for an upcoming dog show. The American Kennel Club website (www.akc.org) lists upcoming events around the country. Look it over with your daughter to choose which competitions and breeds you'll plan to see.

Prior to the dog show, visit your local library and check out some books with pictures of various breeds. Learn about how dogs are trained and cared for and what it takes to be a champion.

⚘ Grow

The dogs at a competitive show are the best of the best. Months of training, grooming, and planning led up to the display you saw today. The judges have determined the criteria for perfection and the dogs have risen to the challenge!

Ask your daughter these questions:

» Do you ever feel pressure to be perfect?
» What do you think a "perfect you" would look like? Act like? Achieve?
» What rewards would there be for being a perfect girl?

It's a blessing that God doesn't ask us to be perfect before he loves us. Romans 5:8 assures us, "But God demonstrates his own love for us in this: While we were still sinners, Christ died for us." Also,

> As a father has compassion on his children,
> so the LORD has compassion on those who fear him;
> for he knows how we are formed,
> he remembers that we are dust. (Ps. 103:13–14)

God doesn't want us to take advantage of his mercy as an excuse to continue in our sin, but we don't have to worry that he'll turn us away or take away his love if we fail.

> For I am convinced that neither death nor life, neither angels nor demons, neither the present nor the future, nor any powers, neither height nor depth, nor anything else in all creation, will be able to separate us from the love of God that is in Christ Jesus our Lord. (Rom. 8:38–39)

It's important we show that same grace to our families and friends. We are guaranteed to have bad moods, show disrespect, and let each other down from time to time. Make a commitment right now to love like Christ: patiently, unconditionally, and forever!

Dear Lord,

Thank you for the chance to see those amazing dogs today. You made some amazing animals for us to enjoy! We're so glad we're not under pressure to be perfect all the time. Thank you for loving us no matter what and being patient with us in our weakness. Help us to give each other that same kind of grace even as we want to be more like Christ every day. Amen!

80

Where in the World?

☞ Grab

» GPS
» Computer
» Small item to exchange

» Camera
» Car keys

Go

Get ready for a high-tech treasure hunt! Check out a couple of websites to learn about the amazing hobby of geocaching. Geo cachingkids.com gives a simple overview of how it works, and geocaching.com will help you choose a cache to search for that's located near you.

Explain to your daughter that someone has hidden a box, or cache, of various items somewhere around your community. To find the cache, numbers describing its location are posted on the internet. You can key those coordinates into your GPS and use the GPS to hunt down the exact spot where the cache is hidden. You will trade in a small item you bring with you for something in the cache once you find it.

Choose your cache location online, keeping the difficulty level and distance in mind, and enter it into your GPS. Have your daughter select her trade-in item, whether it's a bracelet, small toy, or music CD. Be prepared for the outdoors with water bottles, sunscreen, and insect repellent.

Put on your hiking shoes and start hunting! Stop frequently to allow your GPS to reorient its location. When you get close to finding the cache, be patient while you take the time to search the area carefully. Take a picture of your daughter with the cache so you can show it off to family and friends later!

🌱 Grow

You went to a lot of trouble to find that cache today! You had to pinpoint a location, prepare for a hike, and keep searching until you found that treasure. Your reward was more in the memory of the adventure than in the actual item you collected from the box.

God tells us that he searched for us, too. We are his treasure—how incredible!

> For the Son of Man came to seek and to save the lost. (Luke 19:10)

Jesus told two stories in Luke 15:3–10 that explain his heart for those who don't know him:

> Then Jesus told them this parable: "Suppose one of you has a hundred sheep and loses one of them. Does he not leave the ninety-nine in the open country and go after the lost sheep until he finds it? And when he finds it, he joyfully puts it on his shoulders and goes home. Then he calls his friends and neighbors together and says, 'Rejoice with me; I have found my lost sheep.' I tell you that in the same way there will be more rejoicing in heaven over one sinner who repents than over ninety-nine righteous persons who do not need to repent.
>
> "Or suppose a woman has ten silver coins and loses one. Doesn't she light a lamp, sweep the house and search carefully until she finds it? And when she finds it, she calls her friends and neighbors together and says, 'Rejoice with me; I have found my lost coin.' In the same way, I tell you, there is rejoicing in the presence of the angels of God over one sinner who repents."

Dear Father,

Thank you for coming into our world to seek us and save us from our sins. We are so glad we belong to you! Please help us to have the same loving heart you do, and to care about those who are lost without you. We love you! Amen.

Extreme Dates

81

Table for Two

☞ Grab

- » Suit and tie for Dad
- » Fancy dress for daughter
- » Small flower corsage
- » Car keys

Go

Dress up for this special daddy-daughter occasion. Knock on the front door to "pick up" your date. Tell your daughter how beautiful she is and place the corsage on her wrist or dress. Give her your arm and escort her to the car. Open the car door for her and chauffeur her to a fine-dining restaurant or tea room.

When you are at the restaurant, be the perfect gentleman! Open the door for her, take her coat, pull out her chair, and use your best table manners. Choose an entrée from the menu that you wouldn't ordinarily have at home. And of course, order the most decadent desserts the restaurant offers!

> **Dad to Dad**
> Borrow or rent a limo or sports car to make even your drive an amazing memory! If using your own vehicle, make sure it's been polished inside and out. Have classical music ready to play and a flower in a vase in the cup holder.

❦ Grow

Today is all about the best. You are wearing your finest clothes, are using your classiest manners, and have found the most delicious desserts to be had. Also, you're in the best company of all—each other!

God loves us so much that he wants only the best for us too. He says that his plans for us are perfect, his love for us is perfect, and we will spend eternity with him in a perfect place. Read these verses together:

> Old as she was, she still missed her daddy sometimes.
>
> Gloria Naylor

In my Father's house are many rooms. If it were not so, would I have told you that I go to prepare a place for you? And if I go and prepare a place for you, I will come again and will take you to myself, that where I am you may be also. (John 14:2–3 ESV)

And he carried me away in the Spirit to a great, high mountain, and showed me the holy city Jerusalem coming down out of heaven from God, having the glory of God, its radiance like a most rare jewel, like a jasper, clear as crystal. It had a great, high wall, with twelve gates, and at the gates twelve angels, and on the gates the names of the twelve tribes of the sons of Israel were inscribed. (Rev. 21:10–12 ESV)

The wall was built of jasper, while the city was pure gold, clear as glass. The foundations of the wall of the city were adorned with every kind of jewel. The first was jasper, the second sapphire, the third agate, the fourth emerald, the fifth onyx, the sixth carnelian, the seventh chrysolite, the eighth beryl, the ninth topaz, the tenth chrysoprase, the eleventh jacinth, the twelfth amethyst. And the twelve gates were twelve pearls, each of the gates made of a single pearl, and the street of the city was pure gold, transparent as glass.

And I saw no temple in the city, for its temple is the Lord God the Almighty and the Lamb. And the city has no need of sun or moon to shine on it, for the glory of God gives it light, and its lamp is the Lamb. (Rev. 21:18–23 ESV)

Dear Lord,

Thank you for our wonderful time together tonight—it seemed almost perfect! We are so excited about the future you have planned in the place you are preparing for us. We know it will be more beautiful and perfect than anything we can imagine. Give us patience as we wait for you to take us home. Come soon! Amen.

82

Theme Park

☞ Grab

- » Tickets to a theme park or amusement park
- » Sunscreen, walking shoes
- » Water bottles
- » Money

Go

Prepare for your trip to the theme park by pre-purchasing tickets and making your travel arrangements. Keep the weather forecast in mind, as well as any special park events you may want to experience such as fireworks displays or concerts.

Travel to a theme park and grab a park map. Have your daughter point out any rides or attractions that she's excited about. Have an unforgettable day together!

> **Dad to Dad**
>
> *If your daughter's energy or mood starts to fall, boost her up with a water and snack break. Be vigilant about applying sunscreen and consider wearing brightly colored shirts so you're easy to spot in a crowd. Give her instructions for what to do if you become separated. Locate the family bathrooms on your map so she's not left on her own.*

ᛟ Grow

Each park has its own personality, as it orients all of the attractions around a certain theme. Whether it's the down-home Americana of Silver Dollar City, the lovely princesses of Disney, or the oceans of SeaWorld, every park allows its visitors to step into another world for a day.

What is the theme that's running through each day of your life? Are you living out a theme of achieving financial success, finding popularity with your friends, or serving in every way possible in your church? If someone had to describe your number one passion, what would they say?

The theme that God had in mind for us when we were created was to "seek first his kingdom and his righteousness, and all these things will be given to you as well" (Matt. 6:33). When we put our passion for God above everything else, he takes care of our other concerns. We also have this amazing promise: "Delight yourself in the LORD, and he will give you the desires of your heart" (Ps. 37:4 ESV).

Ask each other the following questions:

> » What do I want more than anything else?
> » What do I complain about the most when I don't get it?
> » Which dream or possession would be the hardest to give up?
> » What gets most of my attention and energy in a day?

Answering these questions may give you clues about identifying your greatest passions. Challenge each other to love the One who gives his gifts and dreams to us more than we love those blessings themselves.

Dear Lord,

Thank you for caring about our dreams. Work in our hearts so that our passion is to love you more than anything else. Teach us how to seek your kingdom and your righteousness, and to delight ourselves in you. Help us to love you more than anything this world can offer. Thank you for giving us a hope and a future. Amen!

83

Camping Trip

☛ Grab

» Campsite reservations
» Tent or camper
» Sleeping bags
» Firewood

» Flashlight, matches
» Sunscreen, bug spray
» First-aid kit
» Food (LOTS of food!)

Go

Do a thorough job of packing your food, bedding, extra clothing, towels, and first-aid kit. Nothing will ruin a camping trip faster than being hungry, cold, wet, or sore! Involve your daughter in creating a packing list, and have her check the items off as they're packed into the car. Let her be your navigator with the map as you travel to your campsite.

Have a great time together once you arrive. Set up your tent, spread out your sleeping bags, make a simple lunch, and figure out where the hiking trails and swimming areas are located.

In the evening your daughter can help you lay the firewood for a crackling campfire. Make s'mores, read stories, tell jokes, and rest up after a day in the great outdoors!

> **Dad to Dad**
> *Camping is an awesome opportunity to "unplug." Leave the iPod, Smartphone, laptop, and portable DVD player at home for this adventure.*

〰️ Grow

Camping is one of the best ways to get away from the demands of the everyday. You can take off your watch, turn off your phone and computer, and just enjoy the peace and beauty of the outdoors with your daughter.

Jesus set the perfect example of this by breaking away from the crowds following him to go to the countryside or a mountain to be with his Father. Luke 6:12 describes how "One of those days Jesus went out to a mountainside to pray, and spent the night praying to God." Mark 1:35 tells how "Very early in the morning, while it was still dark, Jesus got up, left the house and went off to a solitary place, where he prayed."

Jesus was continually busy ministering to the people following him.

> Yet the news about him spread all the more, so that crowds of people came to hear him and to be healed of their sicknesses. But Jesus often withdrew to lonely places and prayed. (Luke 5:15–16)

He knew that in our ordinary environment, where everyone "wants a piece of you," it takes effort to have meaningful time with a loved one.

Let's follow Jesus's example and break away to be with our Father just like he did. Brainstorm together to think of a quiet spot you can go to on a regular basis to read the Word, pray, and listen to God.

Dear Lord,

Thank you for teaching us how important it is to spend quiet time with each other and with you. We're so glad you want to be close to us. Help us to remember to take time away from our busy schedules to talk to you and read the Bible. We want to follow your example of making time for the best thing of all—time with our Father. We love you! Amen.

84

It's a Capitol Idea

☞ Grab

» Map of your state government's public buildings

» Money

» Car keys

Go

Find out the tour schedule for your state's capitol building. Check for dates of upcoming special events you may want to experience. Plan ahead and have your driving directions and locations of parking lots, restaurants, your state's museums, and library. Dress in red, white, and blue and travel to your capitol!

🌱 Grow

The idea of government came from God himself. He knew that because of our sinful natures we would often fail at being able to govern ourselves. People can lose their self-control—just look at the cars blowing past you on the freeway! For us to have safe, thriving communities there have to be limits on our choices and behavior. Government is in place to set those boundaries for the well-being of all citizens.

Jesus challenges us to submit to the governing authorities even when we disagree or the rules don't make sense. We are also called to respect those in authority over us because the *role* they fill deserves respect, even if the individual is difficult to admire.

Read these verses together to see what the Bible has to say about government.

Let everyone be subject to the governing authorities, for there is no authority except that which God has established. The authorities that exist have been established by God. Consequently, whoever rebels against the authority is rebelling against what God has instituted, and those who do so will bring judgment on themselves. For rulers hold no terror for those who do right, but for those who do wrong. Do you want to be free from fear of the one in authority? Then do what is right and you will be commended. For the one in authority is God's servant for your good. But if you do wrong, be afraid, for rulers do not bear the sword for nothing. They are God's servants, agents of wrath to bring punishment on the wrongdoer. Therefore, it is necessary to submit to the authorities, not only because of possible punishment but also as a matter of conscience. (Rom. 13:1–5)

> Never think of your children as a burden. They are a blessing! A reward! What could possibly be more satisfying than sending a household of children off into the world to do great things?
>
> Jay Payleitner, *52 Things Kids Need from a Dad*

For in him all things were created: things in heaven and on earth, visible and invisible, whether thrones or powers or rulers or authorities; all things have been created through him and for him. (Col. 1:16)

Remind the people to be subject to rulers and authorities, to be obedient, to be ready to do whatever is good, to slander no one, to be peaceable and considerate, and always to be gentle toward everyone. (Titus 3:1–2)

Dear Lord,

We thank you for the gift of government. We know that you have given us leaders to protect us and uphold the law in our land. Give us hearts that desire to obey the authorities over us. Please bless our government leaders. Keep them safe, give them wisdom, and help them follow you by your Spirit. Thank you for your great love for our community, our state, and our country. Amen!

85

Break a Leg

☞ Grab

» Tickets to a Broadway show
» Car keys

Go

Check out websites such as www.ticketmaster.com to see the theater offerings within driving distance of your home. If traveling to a larger metropolitan area for the production, make hotel reservations for after the show.

Arrive early enough at the theater to enjoy the displays in the lobby, purchase a special program or souvenir, use the restroom, and find your seats. Read through the program with your daughter to discover the names of that night's cast members and a little of the show's history.

ᚖ Grow

Your daughter is probably an experienced actress in her own right, as she has used her imagination in her play for years. Many girls go through a fun stage of playing dress-up and pretending to be a variety of different grown-ups and animals. She has probably played the roles of puppy, mommy, big sister, veterinarian, and teacher with her dolls and friends. This kind of play is wonderful as she dreams about who she will be someday.

Ask your daughter these questions:

» What might you want to be when you grow up?
» What would be fun about that job?
» Where would you like to visit and explore when you grow up?
» What hobbies do you think you might have?
» What kind of home do you imagine living in?

No matter what career, hobby, or home she ends up experiencing, your daughter will always be God's child. She can put her identity in who she is in Christ. The work we do and the things we achieve will pass away—it is our life in the Lord that lasts forever!

Read these verses together:

Yet to all who did receive him, to those who believed in his name, he gave the right to become children of God. (John 1:12)

Therefore, if anyone is in Christ, he is a new creation; the old has passed away; behold, the new has come. (2 Cor. 5:17 ESV)

For we are God's handiwork, created in Christ Jesus to do good works, which God prepared in advance for us to do. (Eph. 2:10)

God has called your daughter his child, has made her a new creation, and has good works planned for her to do. She has an amazing future ahead of her as his daughter!

Dear Lord,

Thank you for giving my daughter a hope and a future. You have given her wonderful gifts and talents, and such a loving heart. Please protect her from sin and those who would try to draw her away from you. Grow her faith and trust in you. Give her a heart that wants to please you more than anybody else. Keep her close to you all the days of her life. We love you! Amen.

86

Can You Hear Me Now?

☞ Grab

» Money
» Car keys

Go

At some point you may decide your daughter is ready to take on the responsibility of her own electronic device. How long has she been begging you for her own MP3 player, cell phone, or handheld video game? Today is the day you make her wish come true!

Prior to your date, shop current sales flyers or internet ads to find out who is carrying the item you have in mind at a price you can live with. Make some calls to confirm that the store you're visiting has the item in stock. Shopping holiday sales or club stores can land you a bundle deal where an extra game or accessory is included in the price.

Have your daughter bring along some of her allowance or birthday money if she'd like to shop for a game or carrying case for her new device.

Once she's made her selection, grab a soda or ice cream together. Help her program phone numbers into her cell phone's contact list, download some favorite songs into her MP3 player, or set up her handheld game system. Take some time to talk through the following ideas together.

⚓ Grow

Electronics can be a blessing and a trial. They can bring fun and convenience, but can also drain a lot of time and attention from more important things. Now is a great time to make your expectations clear.

For a cell phone, talk through these concerns:

» What are your texting plan limits, if any?
» What happens if her phone is lost?
» What time should her phone be powered off at night?

For an MP3 player, talk through these issues:

» Will she have her own online music service to sync her device with?
» Are there any artists or musical genres that are off-limits?
» What are your rules concerning ear buds and protecting her hearing? (See the articles regarding headphones at www. healthychildren.org for recommendations.)
» Are there any other limits, such as no music at the dinner table, etc.?

For a video game, make your expectations clear:

» What game ratings are acceptable for your family?
» How many minutes of game play is she allowed per day?
» Is she required to finish her homework and chores before she plays?
» What safety tips are important for her to follow? (Check out the kids' video game safety articles on www.tweenparent. com and www.childdevelopmentinfo.com.)

For whatever item your daughter selected, make sure you know her school's rules regarding what she is allowed to use on campus and when.

Entrusting your daughter with a new electronic device can be a way to affirm her level of responsibility and maturity. It is also a way to teach simple cause and effect—if she manages her time and usage well she has the reward of using it. If not, she loses the privilege. Ultimately, it gives her the opportunity to learn *faithfulness*. God desires that she grow to be a girl of her word, one who is faithful to respect the value of her possessions and use them in a way that is pleasing to you and her heavenly Father.

Read about the servant's example in Matthew 25:21:

> His master replied, "Good job! You're a good and faithful servant! You proved that you could be trusted with a small amount. I will put you in charge of a large amount. Come and share your master's happiness." (GW)

Dear Father,

Thank you for blessing my daughter with this fun gift today. Please allow it to help her connect with others in new, special ways. Give her the strength to manage her time with it well. Give her a heart that desires to obey by staying within the limits we've placed around her. Please protect her heart from any pride or selfishness that can come from making our possessions too important. May she look at this day and this new gift as coming from your hand and give you all the thanks. Amen!

87

Horsing Around

☞ Grab

» Boots and long pants
» Money

Go

Check out the horseback riding stables in your area. Find out hourly rates, picnic and camping trail ride offerings, and driving directions to the various ranches. Make reservations with a stable that offers guided trail rides of an hour or more.

Before the day of your trail ride, check out some books at the library to explore the world of horses. Find out the different types of horses, the differences between English and western saddles, and what basic terms such as "tack" and "canter" mean. Build anticipation for your date by watching a couple of "horsey" videos such as *Felicity* or *Secretariat*.

At the stable, follow the guide's lead as he or she chooses the right horse for your daughter. They will know which horse's size and temperament make it a good match for your daughter's age and experience level. Take advantage of any opportunities to groom the horses or feed them a treat. Have an unforgettable ride together!

♈ Grow

For most of history, people's primary mode of transportation was their own two feet! Riding on horseback usually went along with a position of status or power.

David declared in Psalm 20:7 that "some trust in chariots and some in horses, but we trust in the name of the LORD our God." He wanted to depend on the power of God, not on the strength of his horses or military.

Brainstorm with your daughter about things you each look to for security, other than God himself. Do you feel better when you have a strong bank account? Health? Lots of friends? Good grades? Read Psalm 121 together:

> Dad, it's not about you. You can't give your kids everything they need anyway. It's about being there, doing the best you can, loving them with all your heart, and then surrendering their lives back to the Creator.
>
> Jay Payleitner, *52 Things Kids Need from a Dad*

I lift up my eyes to the mountains—
where does my help come from?
My help comes from the LORD,
the Maker of heaven and earth.

He will not let your foot slip—
he who watches over you will not slumber;
indeed, he who watches over Israel
will neither slumber nor sleep.

The LORD watches over you—
the LORD is your shade at your right hand;
the sun will not harm you by day,
nor the moon by night.

The LORD will keep you from all harm—
he will watch over your life;
the LORD will watch over your coming and going
both now and forevermore.

Dear Lord,

Thank you for this amazing time riding horses together. Thank you, too, that we can put our trust in your strength. Teach us to trust you more and more. We don't want anything else in this world to become our security—just you! Thank you for your faithfulness to us. Amen!

88

State Fair

☞ Grab

» Water bottles, sunscreen   » Backpack
» Hand sanitizing wipes   » Camera

Go

Plan your day at the fair by checking out the special events schedule and shuttle services ahead of time. Find out about any discount days, kids' day, or concerts that you're excited about. Pre-purchase your tickets to save time and money, and avoid crowded, expensive parking lots by using a park-and-ride shuttle or bus service. Build anticipation for your day by reading about Wilbur's adventure at the fair in *Charlotte's Web* (or just watch the video!).

Once you've arrived at the fair, head to the information desk for a map and a wristband or identification bracelet for your daughter's safety. Make a plan that includes the animal exhibits, midway rides, and food vendors you *have* to try. Make sure to plan for activities each of you will enjoy or one of you will be ready to go home pretty early!

To avoid spoiling your time together with an upset stomach, drink lots of water and order small portions of food to share—quality is better than quantity! Break up the walking by stopping to watch performers or demonstrations throughout the day. Take lots of pictures—you'll want to capture your daughter's smile on the carousel to remember always!

〽️ Grow

Going to the fair is a great way to appreciate the ingenuity and creativity of our neighbors. We get to see where our food comes from and how outrageous food can be! Midway rides can turn our stomachs or give us a bird's-eye view as we round the top of the Ferris wheel.

No one could visit each and every food vendor, see every single animal, or experience every ride at the fair in just one day. That's part of the fun—there's so much to see and do it makes for an unforgettable experience.

We can have the same sense of excitement about the days ahead of us. Who knows what God has in store for us to experience! He has places in mind for us to go, friends for us to meet, things for us to learn, and work for us to do for his kingdom. Life in Christ is exciting and will last forever!

Read Psalm 23 as a prayer to God together:

> The Lord is my shepherd; I shall not want.
> He makes me lie down in green pastures.
> He leads me beside still waters.
> He restores my soul.
> He leads me in paths of righteousness
> for his name's sake.
>
> Even though I walk through the valley of the shadow of
>   death,
> I will fear no evil,
> for you are with me;
> your rod and your staff,
> they comfort me.
>
> You prepare a table before me
>   in the presence of my enemies;
>   you anoint my head with oil;
>   my cup overflows.
> Surely goodness and mercy shall follow me
>   all the days of my life,

and I shall dwell in the house of the LORD
forever. (ESV)

Amen!

Dad to Dad

Dad, the teen years don't have to be scary. When you take the time to invest in your daughter when she's younger, you already have her heart. Your daughter's teen years can be a season of enjoying the fruit of your labor in the early years. The dads of teens I know enjoy "dating" their daughters now—it doesn't require as much planning and they can just enjoy each other's company no matter what they're doing.

Your dates in the teen years are just as important as those you shared when she was little. Even though your daughter is establishing her independence, this is when she needs your guidance and protection the most. Give her space when she really needs it, but stay close by, be available, and make time for both her and the whole family.

20 Great Daddy-Daughter Dates
for You and Your Teenager

1. Go to a music concert of her choice (spring for the concert T-shirt too).
2. Go grocery shopping and cook a meal for the family together.
3. Go to a local coffee shop to enjoy mochas, talking, and a good book together.
4. Try some ethnic restaurants together. If she's studying a foreign language at school, let her help you order off the menu in that language.
5. Saturday morning breakfasts together are the best. Grabbing a coffee on the way to school is also a great time to connect.
6. Go to some of your favorite local sporting events. As one dad told me, "It's not whether your home team wins or loses. It's all about sharing the nachos."
7. Take her to the mall and spoil her every now and then. If you're feeling really brave, take her on an overnight trip to shop in a larger city or at an outlet mall.
8. Check out the museums and cultural attractions in your area.
9. Take your dog for a walk together.
10. Go to a park and rent a canoe or a tandem bike.
11. Pick her up from school and take her to lunch.
12. Do some volunteer work together at a homeless shelter or food pantry.
13. Go through a good Christian book or DVD series together.
14. Take a class at your community recreation center together.
15. Grab a coffee to-go and take a drive in the country. If she's of driving age, let her drive!
16. Take her on one of your business trips. She'll love it! She can hang out by the pool with a good book and her MP3 player while you're in meetings. In the evenings you can grab dinner and see the sights.
17. Take her to a movie or have a video night at home with popcorn and premium ice cream.
18. Take her to a big water park and play. You can forget for a couple hours that she's growing into a young adult that will be leaving home soon!
19. Take your daughter for a manicure and pedicure, and then take her shopping for flip-flops so she can show off her toes.
20. Go through the daddy-daughter dates again. You'd be surprised how many of them, with just a little tweaking, can be used with your older daughter. Plus, you can reminisce about all the memories you created with the dates the first time around.

Resources

Books

Baucham, Voddie Jr. *What He Must Be . . . If He Wants to Marry My Daughter*. Wheaton, IL: Crossway, 2009.

Burns, Jim. *Confident Parenting*. Minneapolis: Bethany, 2007.

Cartmell, Todd. *Project Dad: The Complete Do-It-Yourself Guide for Becoming a Great Father*. Grand Rapids: Revell, 2011.

Casey, Carey with Neil Wilson. *Championship Fathering: How to Win at Being a Dad*. Wheaton, IL: Tyndale, 2009.

Chapman, Gary and Ross Campbell. *The Five Love Languages of Children*. Chicago: Northfield Publishing, 1997.

Clark, Chap and Dee Clark. *Daughters & Dads: Building a Lasting Relationship*. Colorado Springs: NavPress, 1998.

DeMuth, Mary E. *150 Quick Questions to Get Your Kids Talking*. Eugene, OR: Harvest House, 2011.

Dobson, Dr. James. *Bringing Up Girls*. Wheaton, IL: Tyndale, 2010.

Eldredge, John. *You Have What It Takes: What Every Father Needs to Know*. Nashville: Thomas Nelson, 2004.

Farris, Michael. *What a Daughter Needs from Her Dad: How a Man Prepares His Daughter for Life*. Minneapolis: Bethany, 2004.

Johnson, Rick. *That's My Girl*. Grand Rapids: Revell, 2012.

Leman, Dr. Kevin. *What a Difference a Daddy Makes: The Indelible Imprint a Daddy Leaves on His Daughter's Life*. Nashville: Thomas Nelson, 2000.

McBride, James G. Jr. *Rite of Passage: A Father's Blessing*. Chicago: Moody, 2011.

Meeker, Dr. Meg. *Stronger Fathers, Stronger Daughters: 10 Secrets Every Father Should Know*. Washington, DC: Regnery Publishing, 2006.

Payleitner, Jay. *52 Things Kids Need from a Dad*. Eugene, OR: Harvest House, 2010.

Rainey, Dennis. *Interviewing Your Daughter's Date: 8 Steps to No Regrets*. Little Rock, AR: Family Life Publishing, 2007.

Rainey, Dennis and Barbara Rainey. *Growing a Spiritually Strong Family*. Portland, OR: Multnomah, 2002.

Sowers, John. *Fatherless Generation: Redeeming the Story*. Grand Rapids: Zondervan, 2010.

Online Resources

www.allprodad.com

www.betterdads.net

www.dadsanddaughters.org

www.faithathome.com

www.FamilyLife.com

www.familymanweb.com

www.familymatters.net

www.fathers.com

www.Fathers52.com

www.focusonthefamily.com

www.homeword.com

www.strongerdads.org

Rob Teigen has been a publishing professional for more than fifteen years. The author of *Laugh-Out-Loud Jokes for Kids* (under the pseudonym Rob Elliott), Rob met his wife, Joanna, when they were students at Moody Bible Institute.

Joanna Teigen is the stay-at-home mom to their teenage son and three younger daughters. Joanna keeps busy spinning all the plates in their busy household, undertaking freelance editorial projects, and serving at church. The Teigens enjoy church, foster parenting, books, music, and laughter. They live in West Michigan.

Connect with
ROB AND JOANNA TEIGEN

---

www.strongerdads.com

 Stronger Dads · @strongerdads

"If you're a dad with daughters,
you're going to want to read this book."
—**Mark Batterson**,
author of the *New York Times* bestseller, *The Circle Maker*

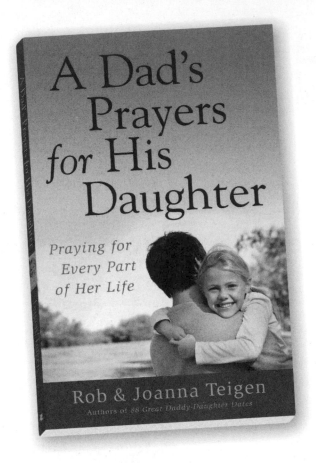

"Rob and Joanna Teigen have written the ideal book
to help fathers pray for their daughters. Want to be a better dad?
Pray for your kids. This book will help."

—**Rick Johnson**, bestselling author of *That's My Son*, *That's My Girl*,
and *Better Dads, Stronger Sons*